ONE
IN A
MILLION

ONE
IN A
MILLION

JULIE MOSS SCANDORA

HARA
PUBLISHING GROUP

To protect the privacy of individuals, their names and other identifying characteristics have been changed. The names and events of my immediate family remain unaltered.

For the sake of simplicity, clarity, and consistency, where a specific person is not indicated, the general parent is assumed to be a mother and the general child, a boy.

Hara Publishing Group, Inc.
P.O. Box 19732
Seattle, WA 98109
425-775-7868

10 9 8 7 6 5 4 3 2 1

First Edition
Printed in the United States of America

Library of Congress Cataloging-in-Publication Data
Scandora, Julie Moss, 1952-
    One in a Million/Julie Moss Scandora – 1st ed.
    p.   cm.
    Includes biographical references
    LCCN 2002116823
    ISBN 0-9710724-6-9
    1. Parenting.   I. Title.
    HQ755.8.S295 2003   649'.1
                            QBI03-200050

Cover Design: Robilyn Robbins
Cover Photo: © 2002 Stefanie Felix
Proofreader: Vicki McCown
Text Design: Stephanie Martindale

Monday's child is fair of face.
Tuesday's child is full of grace.
Wednesday's child is full of woe.
Thursday's child has far to go.
Friday's child is loving and giving.
Saturday's child works hard for a living.
And the child that is born on the Sabbath day
Is bonnie and wise and good and gay.

To my teachers
Rhiannon, Friday's child
Rikki, Thursday's child
Ty, Saturday's child

Table of Contents

Introduction

Seesaw, Sacradown,
Which is the way to London town?
One foot up and the other foot down,
That is the way to London town.

All signs pointed away. Away was obviously where the boy wanted to be – away from this man, away from the computer, away from this situation. Shoulders were slumped, face was turned from the man, and eyes looked everywhere but at the computer screen in front of him. Clearly the boy did not want to be there.

As if his body language were not enough, words erupted to amplify the message. Why did he have to do this? Why could not the man do it himself? Why should he care about this?

The man was no less vocal, but his comments failed to answer the boy's questions. Instead, it was, "Don't be stupid" and "Why are you so lazy?" and "Just do what I say."

I know this man. He is successful in his job, in his dealings with people at work. I know he does not speak in such a way to his clients or coworkers. Imagine telling a coworker to his face that he is a jerk or stupid or lazy in order to get his assistance. No, that does not happen because such methods do not work.

So why does this same person employ such counterproductive measures with a boy? Does he really expect insults to motivate the boy? Does he truly think name-calling will help the boy learn, let alone encourage him to *want* to learn?

Of course not. And had you asked the man, he surely would have agreed that insults do not help in such a situation. In fact, I suggested to the man that there was probably a better way than name-calling to get the boy to do what he wanted. To his credit, the man paused and then adopted a more respectful strategy. Soon, the task was completed with no more complaining and whining by the boy.

This little scene illustrates several points, all of which are the major themes of this book.

First, we need to *be aware of what we are saying and doing* to our children. To get the effect we want, we need to be more conscious of what our words and actions are. In the above scene, had we asked the man what he was doing, he would likely have replied that he was helping a boy learn to use the computer. It is most unlikely he would have replied that he was throwing insults at the child.

Second, we need to *be aware of the impact of our words and actions* on the children in our lives. To know that we are insulting a child is not enough. We must also realize that insults are hurtful no less to a child than to an adult.

Third, *children are deserving of respect.* Because they are little and dependent upon us is no reason to mistreat them. Because they are "merely" children does not mean they should not be listened to. Nor does it mean that their needs (*needs* not wants) should be ignored.

Finally, we do not need special classes or credentialed experts to teach us this. *Each and every one of us has the capability* to figure it out. We are perfectly able to see what our actions are, to realize how they affect others, to understand what our own children need. We can determine what behavior on our part will work best for our children. We may not do it right every time or always at the right time. But the more aware we become of the impact of our words and actions on our children, the closer we get to that ideal.

This book comes from just such observations and endeavors. I have spent years watching children in all sorts of environments – in school and at home, with friends and by themselves, at play and at work. I have stood back and analyzed the situations, comparing my interpretations with others. I have read what the expert and the not-so-expert writers have to say on the subject of child behavior. And I have taken action. Sometimes, my action has been the right one. Sometimes, it has been terribly wrong. And other times, after being wrong, I have corrected my error. Regardless of what I have done, there is always my search for what is really going on – how my words are received by the child, how my behavior affects him, what his behavior is really trying to tell me. Such awareness and the subsequent understanding and appropriate action come with practice.

The purpose of this book is to open our eyes to what we are doing to our children from our children's perspective. It is this understanding of our children and the effect our actions have on them that must come first. Only then can we devise appropriate measures for growing our children into the wonderful adults they are meant to be.

Read. Think. Act.

It is up to us. Our children depend upon it.

Chapter 1

What Do We Want?

Twinkle, twinkle little star,
How I wonder what you are,
Up above the world so high,
Like a diamond in the sky.
Twinkle, twinkle little star,
How I wonder what you are.

Doctor, lawyer, computer programmer. Parents have high hopes for their children. Regardless of individual dreams, the paths mapped out for most are the same: preschool, kindergarten, school, college, and, finally, the job. It is becoming serious business, this child raising. Formalized instruction has filtered down to infants. It is no longer enough to have 12 to 16 years of formal schooling. Children can now look forward to learning to play musical instruments at age three. To ensure reading competency by kindergarten, three- and four-year-olds are taught to read. Good daycares are defined by what their caregivers teach the children in academics, certainly not by how much free time the children have. And, in order to even out the academic preparation of our children, moves are afoot to force preschool upon the economically deprived.

These trends are tied to the belief that academic learning is paramount. It is the key to a successful life.

While most parents have high hopes for their children, such high-salaried jobs are NOT how most parents define a successful life for their children. It is not that they do not want their children to be a doctor or lawyer or computer programmer. It is, instead, that they most want something else for their children. Basically, they want them to be happy and good.

This question – what do parents want for their children? – is just what one writer and speaker on educational issues has asked. As Alfie Kohn frequently talks with parents, he has opportunities for learning what parents have as goals for their children. Here are the answers he received from affluent parents in Texas as related in his *What to Look for in a Classroom and Other Essays*. These parents want their children to be:

> *happy, balanced, independent, fulfilled, productive, self-reliant, responsible, functioning, kind, thoughtful, loving, inquisitive, and confident.* (101)

Almost identical answers were given when he asked the same of parents from an affluent Minneapolis neighborhood. I suspect similar answers would be given anywhere else in the United States.

Notice that nothing was said about their children becoming rich or even comfortable, but instead, "productive" and "self-reliant." Nothing was said about them doing well in school or getting advanced degrees. Instead, it was "inquisitive." Nothing was even said about getting married and having children. Instead, they want them to be "loving" and "kind."

There seems little relationship between what parents want most for their children and what they do to make those desires a reality. They want their children to be happy, yet for the bulk of their childhood, the children are placed in institutions where they are anything but happy. Most children do not want to be in daycare. Most children do not enjoy school. Even for many extracurricular activities, the ones in which parents have decided that their children will participate, the children do not want to be there. Children, for the most part, are not happy on these chosen paths.

Try asking children, maybe not yours, but others' children. Do they like school? Are they happy in daycare? Do they want to play soccer? If they answer as most children answer adults, they will reply that, sure, school is fine, and yeah, daycare is okay, and soccer is good. Children know what parents want to hear. They know that if the right answers are given, the adults will then leave them alone.

So, too, do we adults know, when we really want to know, that that is how the children are answering us. We can tell when it is a quick, noncommittal answer that will get us off their backs. We know because every once in a while we get a different kind of response. There is passion expressed, whether enthusiastically or disapprovingly. The words are many and specific. But it is not just the number of words or the kind of words used. It is how they are used – with genuine feeling. In fact, if a child truly is happy in any endeavor, there is no need to ask because it is so obvious. And that is why those questions about being happy in school or wherever are so tedious to the children. Is it not equally apparent? Of course, they are not truly happy.

This is readily seen by any adult who pays attention. Perceptive teachers do not need to ask their students what they think about school. Listen to one such teacher, Ann Hayes, an eighth grade teacher at Chaloner Middle School in Roanoke Rapids, North Carolina, as quoted by Peter Sacks in *Standardized Minds: The High Price of America's Testing Culture and What We Can Do to Change It.* She says,

> *The kids I teach don't think school is important, and they don't think it has anything to do with what they will end up doing in life. For them, school has always been a punishment they have to live through.* (240)

With few exceptions, children do not enjoy these institutions that have been chosen for them. Some may see them as the necessary path for a job. Some may see them as preferable to an inadequate home life. Some, such as Ann Hayes' students, may see them simply as a path – or punishment – required of all. But are children happy on such paths? No way.

But, "So what?" one might say. Our goal is not necessarily happiness for our children now, but happiness for them as adults. Maybe the end justifies the means. Maybe they must suffer through their childhood to gain in adulthood that happiness and all of those other goals we have for them.

Unfortunately, we cannot ask them if they are happy adults because of the path (daycare, school, etc.) taken; they are still on it. Instead, we must look to those who are done with that part of the journey. We look to those who have the jobs as a result of those years (although not quite as many as we now demand of our children) of institutionalization. We look to ourselves. Are we happy *because* of those years of instruction? Did those years of schooling make us also balanced, independent, fulfilled, productive, self-reliant, responsible, functioning, kind, thoughtful, loving, inquisitive, or confident?

Maybe one or two of those qualities are due to our schooling. But if we are honest with ourselves, we realize that even self-reliance, for instance, is a characteristic we brought to the table ourselves. We had it already or we learned it outside of the institutions forced on us. Many, too, are the adults who have acquired those qualities *despite* the years of their childhood education.

Try asking the question this way. Is our happiness due to what we have done apart from our formal education? Consider where adults derive so much pleasure — from their hobbies and leisure activities. Invariably, these are pursuits that are removed from those 12-odd years of school. Gardening, travel, outdoor adventures, socializing, cooking, sports are high on the list of what adults enjoy. Yet for most, delving into these areas has been apart from the years of formal elementary, high school, and college courses. Classes in those subjects may be taken, but they are outside those schooling years. They are taken for pleasure, not credit. Grades are not a concern; learning is. Just as often, learning takes place on one's own, by reading, experimenting, talking to others who know more. Our happiness comes, then, from pursuing our own interests.

In order to raise our children into the happy adults that we parents want, we do not need to put them through more years of education. Schooling may be a part of the overall plan. But it is too limited to accomplish by itself this grand goal. To bring forth such children, we parents must pursue more encompassing methods. These are under our direct control. Central to them is the requirement to understand our children.

Chapter 2

To Understand

Speak to me, darlin',
    Oh, speaky, spikey, spokey.
Why are those tears
    On your cheeky, chikey, chokey?
Give me the answer
    I seeky, sikey, sokey!
Or else I'll go jump
    In the creeky, crikey, crokey

Some would say it is not necessary to understand the child. It is enough to know what we, the parents, want from the child and just make sure the child meets our wishes. We, as the more experienced and knowledgeable adults, know what is best for the child. Rather than understanding the child, they say, the challenge then becomes figuring out the best way to get the child to obey us.

There are several problems with this approach. First and most obvious is that without a general understanding of children, a parent has no idea what method works best – or at all – to get the child's cooperation.

We may, of course, merely do what was done to us as children. Yet, if we are honest with ourselves, most of us realize that such is not necessarily the best method. Sure, we may have turned out all right. But closer examination will invariably reveal the shortcomings of our parents' methods. The question is not did we turn out all right, but did we turn out all right *because* of those methods or *in spite* of them? Further, if we are really searching for the truth, we will not ask did we turn out all right, but did we become the best we could have because of our parents' child-rearing practices?

For instance, I grew up in a typical middle-class home where Mom was home with the children and Dad worked weekdays in the office. When he came home, Dad was greeted with a litany of all our wrong-doings of the day. Punishments were quickly meted out. We, of course, were fully prepared for this as our mother had told us to "just wait 'til Dad gets home."

I knew enough as an adult that such delayed whacks to our bottoms were totally ineffective for getting the behavior my parents wanted. There certainly was no lessening of our sibling fighting during that time. So I know one method that did not work. But what was to replace it? And even if I thought I knew, what guarantee was there that it would work for my own child?

Which brings us to the second problem with employing discipline of the child without understanding the child: it ignores the individuality of the child. As any parent of more than one child knows, each one is unique. What works for one will not necessarily work for another.

An understanding of children in general and of each one in particular is essential. It is necessary not only for getting the little one's cooperation, but also for preparing the proper path for successful adulthood.

I have read hundreds of books and articles on child raising and child development. This one you hold is one more to add to the list. Yet no advanced learning, no authoritative expert, no definitive book is required for understanding your child. Indeed, you need read no further. I will not tell you anything you cannot discover on your own. All you need is an abundance of time, an open mind, and an environment that includes various children.

The importance of relying on direct experience and observation hit hard as I was in the midst of writing this book. Bruno Bettelheim was an authority and writer I especially respected for his views on child raising. Among his well-known books are *A Good Enough Parent: A Book on Child-Rearing*, *The Uses of Enchantment: The Meaning and Importance of Fairy Tales*, and *Love Is Not Enough: The Treatment of Emotionally*

Disturbed Children. After years of recommending his books without reservation, I chanced upon the book, *The Creation of Dr. B: A Biography of Bruno Bettelheim* by Richard Pollak. The author's research showed that Bettelheim's work and public image were based on fabrications. He was not the degreed doctor with a solid background in child psychology that everyone thought. He had lied about his education, his research, his World War II concentration camp experiences. In fact, he told so many lies that people he worked with never knew whether any of his stories had any truth to them. Nor was he the gentle and kind-hearted man who worked wonders with the children in his care. He harshly blamed mothers for their children's problems in face-to-face meetings. He often lost his temper with employees. He worked to maintain authoritarian control by intimidation. In short, he was hardly the benevolent, well-educated, and trusted psychologist he conveyed in his books and public meetings.

In Bettelheim's works, I had found much material which matched my own observation. Beyond that, he presented other ideas which, although they made sense, did not correspond to anything I had yet observed. How does one then handle such information? What does one think when a formerly well-regarded expert is shown to be a charlatan?

In the end, I had to fall back upon my direct experiences. Those are the true foundations of my beliefs and subsequent practices. That many matched those of Bettelheim was irrelevant. Because an expert agrees with me does not then validate my interpretations. Nor does an expert disagreeing with me make my interpretations invalid. My interpretations rest first on my direct observations and experiences. Interpretations are tested and validated (or not) with subsequent observation and experience. This same procedure is no less so for you, the reader.

The experts have studied their subject extensively, have read profusely, and have discussed the issues at length with colleagues. But no one knows your child better than you, the parent. Your work is not in a vacuum. It does not take place in an ivory tower. You see and deal with your child in countless situations, in various places, with different people. You see far more than does the professional working in limited settings.

In a sense, the revelations about Bettelheim "reduced" him to my level. No longer a credentialed expert, he was just an intelligent adult who often knew what troubled children needed.

So it is with you, the reader. You observe, speculate, try what you think will work. Mistakes are sometimes made but readily corrected. This is the way with those authors whom I most respect. Unlike Bettelheim, they are admired not because of their degrees or education but for their common sense insights. Their writings are derived basically from observing children. What sets them apart from most of us is that, from their observations, they noticed what was going on and made connections that challenged long-held beliefs.

For example, John Holt was one such insightful author. A former teacher, he developed his ideas of how to deal with children from years of interacting with and observing his students and other children in his life. In *How Children Learn*, he talked about a friend, two-and-a-half-year-old Lisa. She was about to pick up a balloon when a gust of wind from the door blew it along the floor. When it stopped moving, she approached it and blew on it, obviously trying to imitate the action of the wind. As Holt noted, this is abstract thinking, usually attributed to children when they are much older, about nine years of age.

Later, Holt told of Danny, also two and a half, who, like many little boys, was an expert in naming different trucks and machines. In this instance, Danny had his favorite truck- and machine-book. He pointed to a picture of a truck and purposely called it the wrong name. He was well aware that it was wrong and took great enjoyment in the joke. Here, the ability to be adept at something yet purposely do it wrong (that is, to make not a mistake but a joke) is also what child development professionals say children can do only when much older.

Alison Stallibrass, in *The Self-Respecting Child: Development Through Spontaneous Play*, talked about her playgroup of toddlers. There were 12 children in a room about 15 feet square. In addition, there was quite a bit of child-sized furniture, including chairs, table, easel, small piano, carpenter's bench, etc. The children were free to walk or run about, even build slides of sorts. Many of the children were often engaged in play upon the floor. Despite all of the physical activity amid the obstacles, the youngsters were rarely involved in collisions or even arguments. These children, even though quite young, were able to be aware of what their playmates were doing and to anticipate their subsequent moves so as not to bump into them. This was possible, Stallibrass felt, because the children were not controlled and, thus, not distracted by adults. Instead, each was able to maintain an awareness of all that was going on – the individual activities of others – and, thus, to fit himself into that whole.

Few teachers or professionals would attribute such awareness and regulation to young children. They would, instead, more likely feel that adult control of the toddlers would be necessary to prevent inevitable accidents – the very ones Stallibrass rarely saw.

To aim to understand the child is truly to run counter to what much of our society tells us. To understand, we approach the child with questions rather than demands. We ask him, for instance, who are you? What do you do? Why do you do this and not that? Do you always do this? Why not? Do others do the same? It is a humbling position for us. We admit we do not know. We seek knowledge. We wish to learn from, of all people, a mere child. That is, we ask the child to teach us.

This is not to be confused with the child directing the parent. The child is not put in charge. He does not rule the parent. We have no desire for tyrants of any age.

I have known children to be put in such a ruling position. They order the adults in their lives about, demanding this, requiring that, doing little on their own. The adults are all too happy to comply. This is indeed a topsy-turvy world. Rather than the adult guiding the child, the child leads the adults. Rather than an adult-centered world, it is child-centered.

What happens to the child in such a situation? At first glance, we might think the child would be thrilled to be in that position, to be ruler of his world, to have power over the adults. But it is, instead, very frightening. A child knows he is but a child. Under normal circumstances, he works to learn from the adults who are more learned in his world. But now they are looking to him. He knows the roles have been reversed, and it is not right.

Put in such a situation, a child retreats further into childhood. He does not grow. Where he would otherwise be learning skills that would take him closer into adulthood – something as simple as learning to tie his own shoes – he is stalled. The adults do everything for him. He does not learn. He remains dependent upon his adults not only because he is not master of even basic skills but also because his definition of self is totally dependent upon the adults always being with him. Where normally in his early years a child relies upon his adults, this dependency is not total; he also is growing in independence and mastering skills, which will allow him eventually to break away. When the tyrant child no longer has his adults to boss around, where is he? Lost. What is he? No one. The children I have seen who are the little tyrants are not happy. In some cases they are babyish, keeping immature speech patterns well after they should have mastered normal pronunciation. It is scary to be in charge of one's world as a young child.

When we work to understand the child, we do not put him in charge of our world. We remain in charge. We use our understanding to better train the child. We adapt what we do and say, what situations we present, what resources we provide so that they are in tune with this unique individual.

In some ways, we become as children, even while maintaining our parental role. John Holt expounded on this. He described how the child is constantly trying to make sense of his world. He approaches his world fearlessly and openly, seeking knowledge, meaning, and sense. This idea is a central thesis in his book *Learning All the Time*. He says of children that:

> At any particular moment in their growth their minds are full of theories about various aspects of the world around them, including language, which they are constantly testing, but not for the life of them could they tell you what these theories are.

(103)

So, bit by bit, a view of his world begins to form. As new information is gathered, his worldview is thus slightly altered. This is not disturbing but expected. He is, after all, working to understand; he realizes that his view must be always open to revision. It is like sculpting in clay. Some clay is added, some is removed, and all that remains contributes to the final form.

Somewhere between childhood and adulthood, that perspective changes. Where once one's purpose in life was to understand the pieces that make the whole, now one looks to interpret life based on a fixed view of the world. Where once one was open to learning all one could, now one closes the mind to any new explanations. Where once one asked, "What does it mean?" now one smugly explains all according to the way it is. To continue the sculpting analogy, it is as if the sculpture is finished. No more need be added; none should be removed; all is done.

Even the great and mighty succumb to sticking to a fixed view of the world. Albert Einstein's extraordinary contributions to science were based upon a specific interpretation of how the universe operated. Throughout his life, Einstein held his set view, looking for a single unified theory which would mathematically explain a relationship between gravitation and electromagnetism. He felt his theory of relativity would be the key. Meanwhile, fellow scientists took his relativity theory and moved on, embracing quantum mechanics, which holds that such a relationship cannot exist because the movement of electrons is not fixed. Instead, their path is best described through probability. Commenting on Einstein's steadfast scientific view, German scientist Max Born said, "Many of us regard this as a tragedy, both for him, as he gropes his way in loneliness, and for us, who miss our leader and standard-bearer."

We parents are no Einsteins. But replacing open-mindedness with close-mindedness, sacrificing inquisitiveness for pat answers, or seeking a simple and final word with no room for fuller explanations does no less damage. What brilliant discoveries were lost with Einstein closing himself off to theories other than ones based on his fixed view? What wondrous possibilities are stifled with us closing ourselves to understanding our own children?

I still remember talking to a father many years ago about his son who was then in high school. The boy was having problems – in school, in his relationship with this man, his father, in life in general – to a degree greater than the average teenager. "Why not," I suggested, "be more open and accepting and understanding?" His reply was a firm "No." The problem, in his eyes, was not a lack of his understanding; it was all in the boy. For all to be right, the boy needed to come over to the father's viewpoint, to accept *his* beliefs, to understand *his* way of living.

These many years later, the situation remains. The boy-now-adult still needs his father's acceptance and understanding. But it is now the son's viewpoint that is fixed: he believes his father will never give him what he needs, so it becomes his turn to reject his father. Here, too, one asks, "What wondrous possibilities have been lost?"

This lack of understanding arises many times when parents see their children disobeying or, in general, misbehaving. What the adults see as flagrant disregard for their rules often is quite a different case. If only they would pause and try to figure out what the child is really trying to say, they would realize the child's intent is far from the evil one they ascribe.

I watched one little boy carefully climb high on some monkey bars. Midway through, his mom discovered him. "Look at what I can do," the boy proudly called to her. "No, Tommy, you know you cannot do that," she replied. Clearly, Mom was impressed not by his accomplishment but by his disobedience. He had been told not to climb the structure, and here he was doing just that. Was he disobeying? That is one interpretation. Another is that the boy was merely showing his mom what he could do. She had said he "cannot" climb it. "Can" refers to physical ability; "may" refers to what is permitted. This is an important distinction, not just a trivial case of semantics. It makes a tremendous difference. Mom had said the boy was physically incapable of mastering the monkey bars; the boy felt he could do it and was showing her in the only way he knew how.

Obviously, the parent was afraid the boy would hurt himself because she felt he could not climb it without falling. When presented with the reality, what could she do? Foremost, she could acknowledge his capability: "Yes, Tommy, I see you *can* climb it." Does she remain fearful, so much that she still does not want him to climb? If, even then, she does not want him climbing, then she must at least recognize it is *her* fear that is operating here and not his climbing ability. So the response becomes, "Yes, you can climb very well. But I am afraid, so for now you will have to come down."

Sometimes, even repeated offenses are merely from a child attempting to communicate, rather than due to a little terror trying to anger the parent. As a mom stood engaged in conversation, her little daughter carried her doll stroller up the building steps. It took a while as the stroller was a bit awkward, although not particularly heavy. Each step was carefully taken; both feet were planted on each step before the next one was begun. Finally, the mother realized what her daughter was doing. "No, you cannot do that," scolded the mom. She took the stroller, put it at the bottom of the steps, and resumed her conversation. The girl then took her stroller and once again mounted the steps. And once again Mom interrupted her conversation, told the girl she could not climb the stairs with the stroller, placed it at the bottom, and returned to speak with her friend. Once more this scene was repeated. This time, in exasperation, the mother swatted the girl for disobeying and removed her and the stroller from the area.

Was this a girl intent on disobeying her mom, for whatever reason? Maybe, but I believe not. The girl was showing through her actions that she most certainly was capable of carrying that stroller up those steps. Trying to convince her mom with words would obviously have been futile. After all, she was primarily engaged in talking with a friend. Further, are not actions far more powerful than words?

When the first attempt does not convince the parent, subsequent ones are tried. Children can be very patient and persistent in this regard. They want to get their point across. "LISTEN TO ME," they seem to scream when their method of communication fails the first time. It is akin to adults talking to a foreigner who does not understand English. Maybe if one *yells* the words the foreigner will be able to understand. Repeated attempts by the child do not lend clarity any better than an American shouting English to a foreigner. Yet our ability to understand what is really going on can be enhanced by pausing. The parent's immediate thought is "What a disobedient little girl!" But, instead, we can ask, "What is my little girl trying to say to me? It must be important to her or she would not keep doing this." Illumination is more likely to enter when one calmly considers the situation and remains open to various explanations. Assuming evil intent closes off any other possible interpretation.

In both of these instances, the parents were acting out of concern for the child. Each was protecting the children from what she felt was possible injury – the boy could slip and fall off the play structure; the girl could become unbalanced or lose her step and fall down the stairs. A parent's job is to protect. But there is a difference between shielding from known hazards, such as poisons or unguarded swimming pools, and denying the exercise of skills.

When a parent prevents the child from challenging his body, far more harm is done than what could happen by giving free rein. A child stretches his limits to learn what he *can* do with his body. He is not on a self-destruct mode. He knows that up until now he could accomplish only this much. Now he wants to know if he can manage a little more. It is stretching a little at a time.

This is the way my children learned to climb a tree. No one pressured them to do it. Nor did anyone tell them that they could not do it or had gone far enough up the tree. Instead, each one climbed as far as she or he felt safe. By trying different trees, they learned which were best to climb. Some have sticky, sappy bark. Some have branches that break easily. Some sway in the wind or bend from the climber's weight more than others. By testing different branches, they learned where the limbs were strongest (closest to the trunk), how far out they could safely venture, and how bendable a branch was with their weight. They never fell. And they have climbed many storeys high in the trees. Sometimes it is for the views, sometimes it is to feel the wild swaying in the wind; sometimes it is to hide during games since no one thinks to look up. And sometimes it is just for the pure pleasure of doing it.

My children have been greatly amused by others' comments when they have been perched in trees a mere 15 feet above the ground. Many children look enviously up at them and point out their presence to their unaware parents. But the parents are not impressed. Instead, they invariably stress to their young the dangers of such play. "Don't you do that. You could fall" are words most often voiced. Certainly, the child does not think so.

To understand the child is to put ourselves in the child's place and be that child. Too often we think we do this, but, mentally, it is still our adult self that is sitting there. We do not remember what it is to be a child in such a position. Instead, we remember how an adult behaves, how an adult thinks, what an adult feels. Adults fear falling; they have farther to fall than do little children. Most adults have lost the flexibility of youth; they have forgotten how to roll in a fall. Adults are big; they cannot fit between the branches of a tree as well as a child.

Adults have had many more experiences than their children. The resulting knowledge can be used to guide children on the proper path. But our experiences can also cause us to instill our unrealistic fears in them. Maybe we were so protected in growing up – because our own parents were afraid of us getting hurt – that we never had the chance to discover what we could do. Rather than test ourselves, we were held back and only told that we could not do such and such. Being raised to fear and avoid risk, we readily teach the same to our children.

Maybe, instead, we experienced the opposite circumstances. Rather than being held back, maybe we were pushed to take risks that we felt were too far beyond our capabilities. Parents who live out their egos in their children subject their children to this. The young ones are pushed to achieve in order to satisfy the parent without regard to what the child likes, wants, or even can do. There is a passage in *Mosquito Coast* by Paul Theroux where the father pushes his son to climb the ship's mast. The boy is clearly afraid but does as his father commands. Getting near the top, he is paralyzed with fear and goes no further, neither up nor down. The ship's crew, disgusted with the father, rescues the boy.

Just as with the child held back, the one pushed beyond is not allowed to discover his limits. There is no opportunity to evaluate or test the risks involved. In the first case, all are rejected as too risky. In the second, all are taken as being surmountable. Neither is true. The child-become-adult who is protected learns to fear all opportunities as unsafe. The one pushed to take all on learns to fear nothing and to leave himself open to unnecessary failure or danger. Neither experience provides the child with the ability to wisely gauge whether he should forge ahead or hold back in a given situation.

Children are not born fearful. They learn to be so. Children fall all the time. That is part of learning to walk and run and skip and jump. Climbing is fun; "hard" never enters into it. Children are very flexible; most adults have stiffened with age and stress. In such situations, children want to know how far they can go. They want to see not what is allowed according to adult rules but what their bodies are physically capable of doing. If they feel safe at just five feet above the ground, they are not about to shoot to the top. They will carefully (if not held by a fearful parent) go just a bit more, enough to slightly stretch their comfort zone.

When the parent denies this exploration and sets the limit, the child then has no idea of his capability. Nor does he have any basis for self-confidence. A child's (or anyone's) self-confidence is derived from experience, from accomplishments, not merely from someone telling him that he is good, strong, a capable tree-climber. These are concepts the child must discover and know for himself. It is only by doing – by being allowed to do – that they come about.

In working to understand the child, we benefit by having the perspective that there is a valid reason for the child doing what he is doing. This does not equate to condoning inappropriate acts. Rather, it means we realize why the child has acted as he has. Our subsequent response will invariably be far different with such understanding than if we merely respond to the child's overt wrongdoing.

For instance, when my son was about four years old, the late afternoon brought an unfortunate ritual. His dad would come home, worn out from work. He would pat the dog, change clothes, then exercise in his work-out room until dinner time. After seeing his dad go in to the work-out room, Ty would kick the dog.

Clearly, kicking the dog was wrong. Less clear was why he was doing it. Highlighting these few events has made the explanation more obvious. But at the time, I could have strung any number of events together or come up with numerous explanations. By sitting back and looking at life from Ty's perspective, I gained insight to his behavior: not only did Ty need time and attention from his dad but he needed at least as much as the dog was getting. Ty was angry because he was ignored by his dad. He was further upset because the dog got more than he did. So it was only natural to take his anger out on the dog.

When one sees a child old enough to know better mistreat the family pet, the immediate reaction is to scold, tell him not to do that, remove him from the situation, put him in time out. While this addresses the wrongness of his action, it does nothing to ensure it is not repeated. The scolding and subsequent punishment are based on the assumption that (take your pick) the child does not know any better, the child lacks empathy, the child is just mean. The reality is another matter. In our case, it was that the child needed attention from his dad, a far cry from what any outside observer would have thought. If the real cause is not addressed, the inappropriate action will remain or get worse. Or if denied that outlet, another seemingly unrelated response will arise. By understanding the child and responding appropriately, two things happen: the child's needs (here, time with Dad) are satisfied, and the inappropriate action (in this case, kicking the dog) stops.

Parents who try to be understanding sometimes take the tactic of talking to the child. They seek understanding through conversation. So the child is asked why he did whatever. For children, this is as ineffective as addressing only the overt act. Little children rarely know why they act as they do. (Teenagers are often not much better. And even adults have trouble identifying the true reason for their actions.) Such introspection is beyond them. Nor do they have the vocabulary to explain. It is just beyond a four-year-old's capability to say, "I kicked the dog because I am angry at Daddy for not spending any time with me." That will not happen. To question a child is to put him in deeper distress. Not only has he done something wrong (kicked the dog), not only does he feel miserable (he has this unarticulated need to be with Daddy), but now he has questions for which he has no good answer. When put in such a situation, the child will do whatever he can to escape it. Best in his mind is to give an answer that the questioner will accept. Why did he kick the dog? The answer will invariably be along the lines of "I don't know." It is a truthful response and often the first one given. It usually sends the parent into exasperated tirades: "If you don't know why you do it, then DON'T DO IT." Usually such a response is insufficient, so the child digs to come up with something that will be accepted. So we hear "Because I don't like him" or "He was going to bite me" or anything that will end this uncomfortable questioning. In the end, we are no better off. The true reason for the action eludes us, so the behavior will continue, as will the unfulfilled need.

Casual conversation, however, can be a most revealing means of learning what is really going on with the child. But here, too, understanding, patience, and openness to what is being expressed are necessary. It can be as challenging to interpret the child's words or true meaning as any inappropriate actions.

When we were still working with getting enough Dad-time for Ty, my husband, Keith, went on a business trip. I told Ty that his dad would be home soon and would spend Saturday with him. "What," I asked, "would you like to do with Daddy?" "Cut him up in little pieces" came the reply. I did my best to repress my shock and horror. What a nasty statement for a son to say about his father! Yet that immediate response is merely the superficial interpretation. Pausing tells us more. It says that this is a very important issue to get such an outrageous answer. It says there must be much pain felt by the boy that he reacts by wanting to inflict pain on another. Most of all, it gets attention and says, "Help me."

Again, to react to such a response by decrying the boy's answer is an injustice. In his eyes, the words are right. They show how hurt he is, how important time with Dad is, how desperate the situation is. To punish him for them is to deny his real need. To expect him to notice that need is to ask the impossible. He feels the pain. He has not the introspective capability to put words to the pain or to describe its source.

Such behavior, verbal or active, requires an adult response. Above all, we must believe the child is behaving appropriately in his eyes. We must then ask, not disbelieving or aghast, but open-mindedly, in what way that behavior is appropriate to him. What is he trying to say? What is going on in his life that can be connected to this? We, as the wise adult, must think and analyze and, ultimately, help him. His actions loudly call for just that: help. This is a helpless child who needs his adults to figure out what is wrong and how to make it right. Here is where putting a child in charge or creating a child-centered world would fail. The child would not know to ask (demand) that the father spend more time with him. Since such articulation is beyond him, his words or actions would still appear inappropriate. Being lord over all would not help him get what he needs. It is the adult, wiser and more experienced, who must be in charge in order to help.

These events in Ty's life stood out. They were aberrations. Ty did not normally hurt animals nor want to inflict pain on others. It was clear that something was wrong because these happenings were abnormal both for Ty specifically and for children in general.

But what is normal or abnormal, common or uncommon, natural or unnatural? Because certain behavior in children is common is not to say it is natural. The well-known pediatrician and author T. Berry Brazelton, in *To Listen to a Child: Understanding the Normal Problems of Growing Up*, believes we should not worry about certain problems of childhood since all children go through them. This same logic says one need not worry, for instance, about the humiliation, suffering, and danger that some college students go through in fraternity hazing because all new members of the fraternity go through the same process. Such problems (or hazing or whatever) may well be common. But are they normal?

Brazelton includes bedwetting, thumb-sucking, and reluctance in going to school as typical problems for young children. But even calling them common is not totally true. They are common in Western societies, not in indigenous societies. What is it about our culture that our children develop such problems where children in other cultures do not?

In his *Baby and Child Care*, Benjamin Spock saw bedwetting as common, more so in boys, but certainly not natural. He identified several explanations for it. Most were related to stress or feelings of inadequacy in the child. For instance, a major change, such as a move to a new house or the arrival of a new baby in the home, could bring it on as could an exciting or a frightening event.

The point is, this common problem is not natural and, instead, indicates something is wrong in the child's life. "Wrong" here does not mean that we must necessarily change the situation to make it "right" for the child. Certainly, we are not going to get rid of the new sibling because the older child does not want a competitor/baby in the house! Instead, it indicates the child's perspective. We now understand the reason for the unnatural (but possibly common) problem. So, in such a case, we look to answer the deeper needs. We make sure the older child gets some individual attention. Or we show him how to help with the baby. Or we give voice to how much more competent he is than his sibling and how he will be able to teach the baby so much. We look for ways to relieve the stress he is feeling in having a new baby around.

Each child is unique. The reason for one child's bedwetting is not necessarily the same for another. As always, we must look at the child's life. What is going on? What is different (if the bedwetting has not always been present)? Are there other problems going on at the same time? To treat this as something that many children just go through is to do injustice to the child. It ignores his cry for help. And in this case, especially, it keeps the child burdened with an embarrassing situation.

So it was with my son, Ty. Although he was completely toilet trained in one day when he was two and a half, one year later he began wetting his bed. Previously, he had had isolated instances due to scary movies or frightening stories. But this was different. It started innocently – also an isolated occurrence – but then grew until it was happening almost every night. Clearly, something was wrong. What was different in Ty's life that might be responsible? After much thought, I realized what he was trying to tell us.

Both my husband, Keith, and I had been working full-time while Ty was in daycare. Now I was home all day with Ty. With that change, Keith felt less of a need to be involved in home affairs. In addition, Keith was taking more overnight and extended business trips. The combination of more Mom and less Dad created a need in Ty for a better balance with more Dad. Once Keith started giving Ty more of his time, Ty's bedwetting disappeared.

There is absolutely no way Ty could ever have explained why he was wetting his bed. And no device that might have rid Ty of the problem would ever have addressed his real need: time with Dad. By discovering the reason for his "common" problem, I eliminated both the source and its manifestation. To have assumed otherwise, that this was a problem that could not be solved would have left an important need unfilled and an embarrassing and inconvenient situation intact.

What about thumb-sucking? While our culture accepts this as normal for infants and toddlers, adults find its practice most disturbing in older children. So what is natural here?

Babies are born to suck (actually suckle, but I will use the more commonly used term). They need to do so to survive. In native cultures that allow breast-feeding on demand and that keep the infant in constant contact with his mother, thumb-sucking is virtually unheard of. (See, for instance, *The Continuum Concept: Allowing Human Nature to Work Successfully* by Jean Liedloff.) In our culture, breast-fed babies tend to thumb-suck less than their bottle-fed counterparts. If one believes the sole intent of feeding the infant is to get food into him, then thumb-sucking in infants is not seen as a problem. The bottle is merely more efficient in dispensing the milk, so a need to suck remains. If one believes feeding an infant is more than a physical activity, then thumb-sucking may indicate that other needs are not being met. For instance, providing more time at the breast may give the infant a stronger bond to the mother and make him feel more secure. We cannot ask the infant what is going on. We must use our skills of observation.

We must also bear in mind what we want in our children. How we treat the child, what we do to him, what experiences we provide for him all play a part in the development of his personality. For instance, in the United States, parents tend to want children who are highly independent. Infants who learn to comfort themselves by sucking their own thumbs rather than seeking comfort and security at Mother's breast learn early on to rely upon themselves. In such cases, while thumb-sucking is not normal across cultures, it is consistent with what Americans want in their children.

It must be added, however, that cultures that breast-feed and maintain constant physical contact with infants have children who are also self-reliant and self-confident. Infants sleeping with their parents at night and kept in a sling on their mothers' hips during the day do not make for dependent children. Nor do they grow into dependent adults. American parents' behavior may be consistent with the desired end-result, independent children, but our methods are obviously not the only means to that end.

What of the older child where breast-feeding or bottle-feeding is no longer an issue? Here, thumb-sucking is another matter. Infants who have never thumb-sucked do not do so when older. It is only the children who experienced it as infants who later use it for comfort. While not natural, is this, nevertheless, a problem? Again, we must understand the child. In our society, which places a premium on independence, children are often expected to fall asleep on their own, in their own bed, in their own bedroom. Alone and cut off from the rest of the family, which is the child's security, these children often need something to comfort them at bedtime. Thumb-sucking can provide this comfort. When else does thumb-sucking occur? Is it during times of stress or fatigue? Is it only at specific times, say, when introduced to a stranger, when with certain people, at certain times of the day? Thumb-sucking can provide the means for a child to comfort himself during such times. But it can also indicate that something more is going on. For instance, if it happens only when the child is with a certain person, we would ask, "Why? What is going on between the child and this person that causes the child to retreat to thumb-sucking for comfort?" Here, too, it is up to us to delve into the matter.

Thumb-sucking is not natural. But it is common in our culture. For the most part, it is not a problem. Usually, it is an indication of the de-emphasis upon breast-feeding and an emphasis upon independence in our society in general and the child's family in particular. Less frequently it is an indication that something is dangerously upsetting in the child's life. In such situations, it is then our challenge to discover the cause.

The third "typical" problem for young children, reluctance in going to school, is obviously not a problem in indigenous societies. There, learning is part of everyday life, not separated and segmented from it. Can such reluctance in our society then be called natural? It is certainly common.

Reluctance takes many forms. It can be faked or imagined or a real illness. Stomachaches or headaches are common manifestations of a child's aversion to school. Sometimes it is just a vocal "I don't want to go to school." It can become more extreme with tears and strong protests. It can become more subtle with delay tactics – eating breakfast at snail speed, lying in bed past wake-up calls, forgetting crucial items at the last minute.

How one responds to such reactions to going to school depends upon the individual child. As always, it requires an understanding of the child and what he is really trying to tell his adults. Is he especially afraid of the unfamiliar? Does he feel inadequate or unable to measure up? Is he especially shy or small or young for his class? In such instances, the child needs help confronting these fears and obstacles, which he can overcome.

Sometimes, there is more behind the child's protests. I know of one girl who went to kindergarten every morning in tears and came home every afternoon in clothes torn. It was, her mother said, as if she wore a sign: please beat me up. Indeed she was, every day for the first several weeks. Whether the parent allows the child to be subjected to such treatment will depend. This mother felt she had no option. She had to work, could not afford private school, and could not get her child transferred.

Most of our children do not experience such extreme physical treatment in school. But that does not make their reactions any less valid. The adult must be perceptive. Is the child bored? Is he verbally abused by the teacher or by fellow students? Is he at a loss for what is going on in the classroom because he cannot see the chalkboard? There are innumerable possible explanations. The important part is to realize that what the child is trying to tell the parent is real to him. If nothing else, his opinion must first be accepted. Only then can the adult decide whether action is to be taken to change the child or to change the environment.

There are always options available. One need not merely accept the status quo. What does it say to the child when one sends him day after day to an environment that is hurting him, when one knows this is the case, and when the child knows the parent knows? Is not one of the parent's basic responsibilities to ensure the child's safety from obvious harm? What about verbal abuse? Is it right to expect a six-year-old to deal with that, let alone even to know how?

The little girl who was daily beaten up in school has grown into a fine young woman. The abuse did not make her mean. The experience did not make her hate her mom. Her mother had acknowledged her daughter's response but explained that there was no choice for her; the girl had to learn to deal with the other children.

We must look deeper than the superficial. We need to pause, observe all that is happening, and be aware even of seemingly unconnected events. Most of all, we must be willing to examine how we ourselves might be a part of what has happened.

Time and again, this is what happened with one little boy I know. His dad would ask, for instance, "Who wants to go to the hardware store?" "I do, I do!" would pipe up the little voices of his son and the son's friend, Max. "Okay," the dad would respond, "Max and I will go." His son's voice was loud and clear; his response, obvious. But the father ignored him. Not only did he ignore him, but he also gave special attention to the friend over his own son. Is this a kind and loving way to treat anyone, let alone one's own child? Is it any wonder that the boy would respond to his father's teasing by hitting him? Certainly hitting one's parent is not good. But does the father ever speculate on his role in the sequence of events? Does he truly believe that this action on his son's part arises spontaneously, that it is unconnected to any other event, and that it is due to evil intent? How can he be so blind to his own direct contribution to the boy's behavior? How can he be so mean? And why does he refuse even to try to understand?

Such encounters are painful to watch. My heart goes out to the little boy. He has a good heart and is never mean to anyone (yet). Such teasing by his dad will surely test the boy's limits. It is bad enough that the boy is thus mistreated. It goes further. He is punished for acting out against his father. So, as happens all too often, the reason behind the behavior is hidden, the cause is unaddressed, and the true perpetrator goes free. How will such events play out in time? Do these many little mistreatments gradually accumulate until the child, overloaded and unable to take any more, explodes with an action far worse than a mere swat at his dad?

The boy's family is a "nice" one. The parents want only the best for their son. They realize time with him is important so give him much. They give him many opportunities for playing outdoors. They are very involved in his organized activities and are active in the community at large. He does not want for material comforts. Yet this teasing is a very real part of the boy's life with his dad.

Such meanness by adults is not uncommon. One time, Ty and a friend were climbing a tree. The father started tickling Ty as he was hanging by his hands from a branch. After a point, the tickling, despite cries to stop, became too much. Ty let go and fell. Fortunately, he was not hurt. What is the point in such behavior by adults? Is it fun to watch a child fall from a tree? Does one feel powerful in so controlling a little one? Where is the sense? How, in even a small way, does it teach something positive to a child? Clearly, in this case as with the previous one, the adult has problems which are being manifested in his behavior with children. But that certainly does not excuse him.

How oblivious this man is to the results of his actions became clear a short time later. When I was told about the tickling incident, I forbade Ty to play at the boy's house when the father was around. Unfortunately, I had not been sufficiently encompassing in my rule. A few weeks later, Ty was playing at a park with the boy and his dad. They were playing a chase game, but the father did more than chase. He would fill the children's boots with wet sand whenever he got the chance. When they would stop to empty the boots, he would push the children into the mud. Although the children told him to stop, he continued.

This time, I confronted the man. He was sincerely sorry. But his remorse was not due to having hurt or taken advantage of the children. Instead, he was sorry for having upset me! The children mattered not. He did not understand them, did not comprehend how his behavior affected them, did not respect them as individuals worthy of proper treatment. I, an adult, being upset mattered more than children being abused. Just to hammer in his point, as we were leaving, he looked at Ty and said in an attempt to be funny, "Look at what you did. You got me in trouble." Still clueless, he believed that it was the child who was at fault for tattling, not the adult for hurting. Fortunately, Ty was not convinced. "You did it yourself. You got yourself in trouble" was his reply. At least one in the party understood what was going on.

I have cited several instances of children misbehaving. Where the children were listened to, where time was taken to consider reasons for the behavior, where understanding prevailed, the children were helped. The unacceptable behavior – kicking a dog, bedwetting – stopped. Approaching the events with understanding did not spoil the child. Nor was the parent seen disrespectfully by the child.

Where the children and events were approached without understanding, the children were not helped. The one boy still hits his father when angered. And he has found even more ways to get back at his dad. The boy whose father was mean to Ty behaves similarly with his son. Their relationship suffers also.

Without understanding, the underlying problem remains. The child suffers. The parent is ineffectual at best, unreasonably punitive at worst. It is a lose-lose situation.

By understanding the child and taking appropriate action, everyone wins. The child's problem is validated and usually solved. His behavior improves. And the adult maintains respect through successfully dealing with the problem. This is the point that needs emphasizing. Understanding the child does not lead to further misbehavior or to disrespect for the parent. It is just the opposite.

Chapter 3

To Respect

Fishes swim in water clear,
Birds fly up into the air,
Serpents creep along the ground,
Boys and girls run 'round and 'round.

Without respect there can be no understanding. We must see the child as a unique individual, apart from ourselves, before we can come close to understanding what he does and why he does it. Yet this seems so hard to do. We have trouble understanding even on the most mundane of levels. *We* are cold, so we tell the *child* to put on more clothes. But the child is fine; it is we who are cold. So who are we really dressing? What does *our* response to the weather have to do with what the *child* wears? Do we not want the child to listen to his own body to know whether he is hot or cold, hungry or satisfied, tired or energized, or whatever? That is the only way he can properly respond.

I do not know how many Halloweens the children suffered through, sweltering in their costumes. It was definitely too many, they tell me. The nights were cool and damp, so I made sure they had plenty of clothing on under their trick-or-treat outfits. Unfortunately, they knew what I did not comprehend. Running or even walking up so many steps, to so many houses, along so many blocks kept them plenty warm. Bundling up was not only not necessary; it also made them most uncomfortable. Finally, I learned and let them decide how much extra clothing to wear. It was only years later when I delivered flyers to the 40 or so houses in my two-block area that I personally understood. Until then, I only heard the children's words. ("We'll be warm enough, really, Mom.") After walking up and down many five-step walkways, I experienced firsthand what they had been trying to explain to me all of those years: one gets plenty warm just going from one house to another. And I had not traveled nearly as long or as far as the children had on Halloween.

We are not always fortunate enough to experience exactly what the child is going through. Individual bodies respond differently to the same conditions. For instance, in our house in the daytime, we set the thermostat to 63° for the winter. On a typical winter day, household members will display a wide spectrum of dress in response to this temperature. Daughter Rikki will be barefoot in shorts and a sleeveless top. Rhiannon will have jeans, shirt, sweater, and socks. Keith will have light sweatpants, long-sleeved shirt, and wool slippers as he tries to turn down the thermostat even lower. Add to this array any visiting friends from a typically balmy 70° house, and they will be fully and doubly clothed. Reactions to the same environmental conditions vary greatly.

We cannot expect all to react as we do. Instead, we need to respect the other, be he adult or child. This means we listen to what the other has to say and honor it. This certainly does not mean doing only what the child wants. It is one thing for a child playing outside to say he is warm while we shiver. It is quite another for him to refuse a raincoat for the walk in the park because the sun is shining now while we can see the approaching rain clouds. To listen is not necessarily to give in to his side. It is to hear it and to consider it, then to respond appropriately.

Sadly, many do not even think of listening.

It was a beautiful summer day in early July. But the voice was anything but beautiful. The woman was yelling and yelling and yelling. This is not what we normally hear on our street. After the first minute or so, I went outside to investigate. A very angry woman was climbing out of her car and advancing toward one of the neighborhood children. The verbal onslaught continued. The poor child was in tears, apologizing, but the woman would not let up. By then, I had had enough.

I told the woman to stop, that the child was sorry and had said she would not do it again (although I had no idea what "it" was).

Hours later, the woman and the girl's mother had a talk. This is what had happened. The girl had been tossing "snap pops" onto the sidewalk. These are little balls of gunpowder, perfectly legal, that make a sharp pop sound when squeezed or hit against something hard. Although available year round, they are heard much more often around the Fourth of July. They are one of the few legal "fireworks" that children can safely use. The girl had chanced to throw a snap pop down as the woman's car had gone by. She had not tossed it at the car, had not tossed it in the street, but merely had thrown it on the sidewalk as she had been doing all along. The woman, however, thought a rock had been thrown at her car. So she had immediately launched into her tirade against the child. Never once did she even consider the possibility of the circumstances being other than what she assumed them to be. She had seen no rock fly; there were none in the street; her car had no new dings. Yet she remained firm in her interpretation. Not once did she, even angrily, ask the poor girl what she had been doing.

Had the woman paused (count to 10, inhale deeply, exhale slowly . . .) and listened to the child, a most different series of events would have ensued. She could have seen the snap pops, had a demonstration of how one works, and heard what it sounds like. She could have talked to the child and learned that no evil was intended. Then a child would not have been humiliated unnecessarily. An adult would have been enlightened, maybe even have formed a less suspicious opinion of youths. Anger would have been dissipated. And understanding would have prevailed. Such did not happen, all for the want of respect for a child.

This point was illustrated in the Sunday comics awhile ago. In the strip *For Better or Worse*, a little girl, walking with her father and grandfather, sees a raccoon up in a tree. The girl points it out to the adults, but neither one sees it, neither one believes her. Finally after looking at the tree for some time, one of the adults sees the animal. The other adult is then convinced. Why, wonders the girl aloud to these men, are adults believed in such a situation, but not children? Why, indeed? Or, as I would ask, why are children given so little respect? Why do adults assume that only they can see clearly, figuratively and literally, while children cannot?

My daughter had a similar experience with a friend and his family. We have always been free about letting the children use people-powered tools. Proper usage is demonstrated to them, and after we see they handle the tool properly, they are on their own. Not all parents believe this is safe, and that is fine for us; we do not impose our practices on them or their children. But sometimes such families have rules about tool usage that do impact our actions. Still, we can adjust and do as best we can. Or so we think.

Rikki was using her pocketknife. Her friend was not allowed to play with any knives. In fact, he had been told he could not even be near anyone who was using one. In respect of this rule, Rikki sent the boy to the far corner of the yard as she showed another friend what she was doing.

Later, the boy's parents heard he had been present when Rikki was using her knife. As a result, she was forbidden from playing with her friend for a week. Never did the parents ask for Rikki's side of the story. Never did they even talk to her about it – only the son was told the consequences. When I explained to the parents that there was no intent on Rikki's part to go against the rules, that she had in fact made allowances for the rules, and that if that was not enough they needed to be more specific with their rule (exactly how far away must he be?), they were unyielding. This information did not matter. They had decided on a punishment, and it would stand. They could not admit they were wrong.

Yet by remaining steadfast in light of a fuller picture of what happened, they end up making more mistakes.

In the diary and biography of Opal Whiteley (*The Singing Creek Where the Willows Grow: The Mystical Nature Diary of Opal Whiteley with a Biography and an Afterward by Benjamin Hoff*), similar circumstances show that such actions rarely teach what we intend. Opal was an extraordinary girl, especially in tune with her natural world and very sensitive to those around her. As a six-year-old raised in an Oregon logging community, she had a typical load of chores to perform. In addition, she tried to go beyond what was required of her and help her mother further. Her story is a bittersweet one of, among several themes, her misguided attempts to help.

For instance, a flour sack that was to become Opal's underskirt was drying on the clothesline. Her mother muses that she wishes she knew of a quicker way to get the printing off of the sack than by repeated washings. After her mother leaves, Opal comes up with a quicker way: snip, snip with the scissors and it is all out of the flour sack. When her mother comes home, Opal runs excitedly to her to tell her it is out. But her mother:

> . . . looked no glad looks. She did only look looks about for a
> hazel bush. First one she saw, she did take two limbs of it.
> All the way to the door, she make tingles on me with them. I
> do not think she does have knowing how they feel — such queer,
> sore feels. (150)

Another time, Opal churns the butter. Her mother then pats the substance into its proper form and, as she tosses the butter paddle onto the table, says she hopes never to see it again. Taking her mother literally, Opal later tosses the paddle into the nearby creek. Not long after, her mother spanks her, has Opal retrieve the butter paddle, and then spanks her again. Opal writes about her confusion, wondering why in the world her mother had said she wanted *never to see the paddle again.*

No less does she wonder about why she is spanked. This comes out when Opal gets creative with the "china mending glue guaranteed to stick." Her mother has patching and mending of clothes to do all of the time. Opal sees that the patching is a bother for her mother, so when her mother leaves one day, Opal does the week's mending with the glue.

Upon her return, her mother discovers most of the glue is gone and questions Opal. After explaining all, Opal gets spanked. But unlike most such instances, her mother tells Opal the reason for the spankings. They are "to be good on." Opal is glad to hear that because usually:

> I don't know what I get spanked for. And I do like to know,
> because if I did have knows what I was spanked for, I'd be real
> careful about doing what it was again. (205)

Again and again, Opal tries to help, and all she gets are spankings. Never is it explained exactly what she has done wrong and why she is given the spankings. Her mother knows why she spanks but assumes both that Opal has purposely done wrong (there is that evil intent, again) and that she knows why she gets spanked. She sees no need to explain anything to Opal. But she is mistaken on both accounts. As Opal herself says, she cannot change her ways if she does not know what she has done wrong. I suspect, too, that even had her mother known that Opal's intentions were good, the spankings would have continued. One gets the feeling, even from Opal's point of view, that the woman is not only exasperated by Opal's continual mistakes or mischief but also worn out by the physical labors of raising a family in the wilds of Oregon. Her patience seems very thin.

Yet how much less exasperated might she have been had she truly helped Opal understand what she was doing wrong? And how much more patient might she have been if she had understood that Opal, far from having any evil intentions, was really trying to help? Instead, there was no respect for Opal, no listening to her, and no understanding of her behavior. To her mother, it was obvious: the girl was bad and required tremendous energy on her mother's part to get her to behave.

In such a world, the intent is to have the child obey the parent. It is irrelevant whether the parent is right or wrong, so there is no need to discover if the parent has made a mistake. Obedience is all. There is no room for interpretation by the child of the parent's decision. Respect by the child for the parent's rule must be absolute. It does not matter that the parent's action is based on incomplete or incorrect information.

How is a child to behave under such circumstances? Even when one is obeying or believing to obey the rules, one may be wrong and, thus, punished. How does that teach the child to follow the rules? And, more important, what exactly does it teach the child?

It teaches the child much, but not necessarily what we think. For one, it teaches the child to withhold information. If his view of the situation is different but will not be listened to or considered, there is no point in his mentioning it. This may not much matter if we are intervening in yet another altercation with his sibling. It will matter if it happens often enough so that he just automatically closes off sharing anything with his parents. There are times when we do want our children to be forthcoming. We want them to be open with us and share their opinions and ideas and concerns. But if we give them the feeling that if their views differ from ours, then their opinions do not matter, they will have no reason to open up to us. What is the point if they will receive no support?

For another, it teaches the child that the parent is always right. Further, this "rightness" is based not necessarily on logic or fairness, but on power. It teaches that one does not admit making mistakes, for that would diminish one's power. Upon what would this superior position rest if every decision were open to question? No, obedience must be absolute. And it teaches one to seek power since fairness and justice cannot prevail where one is not listened to, where the other side of the story is ignored.

It is a sad world where a child is not listened to, where decisions are handed down without regard for hearing all sides and reaching a fair interpretation, when parents feel safe only when their rule is absolute. Parents want respect, yet this behavior does not generate respect. At best, it brings strict obedience. But that lasts only as long as the parents' power is felt. What happens when the child gets older or bigger or moves away? How can this power still hold them?

Try seeing this from the child's view. His parents maintain that they are always right. Yet the child *knows* that there are instances when this is not so. He is not blind. He is not stupid. Yet he cannot discuss these differences with his parents. No true discussion with listening to both sides can result. It is only a lecture where he is told that their way is the only way. So what can he do, knowing that the image they are trying to impose on him is false? He has no choice but to hold back. He keeps his opinions to himself. But this secrecy readily transfers to other secrets. Problems he has, trouble he gets into, questions that naturally arise as he copes with growing up – all of this he will want to hold to himself. After all, he knows full well what his parents will say. Why bother going to them?

The natural result of this is a situation described by Brad Blanton in *Practicing Radical Honesty: How to Complete the Past, Live in the Present, and*

Build a Future with a Little Help from Your Friends. A young woman had had an abortion when in college but had never told her parents. She feared their wrath because she knew they did not approve of premarital sex. Yet when she finally did tell them, it was not anger that came to the forefront. More than anything, they expressed their regret in not having been able to help their daughter when she had most needed support.

When we tell our children that we are always right, we leave little room for them to explain or even share their wrongs with us. When we claim not to make mistakes, we create an image no child can live up to. When we say our way is the only way, we create a rigid system that will be inadequate in the changing world in which we live.

But more than anything, when we create these images of perfect, always-right parents, we do the greatest injustice to our children. We lie. It is only a matter of time before we are found out. Is that truly the image we want to present to our children? Is that the example we wish to set? Do we really want to tell them that lying is okay as long as the liar is in a position of power?

Is that how one gains respect from her children, by lying to them? And is that how one shows respect for her children, by lying to them?

Consider respect derived in another way. Consider a parent who is patient and listens to the child, a parent who seeks fairness, a parent who admits to mistakes. Will a child feel insecure because the parent might be wrong? No, he will feel safe knowing that fairness is the aim.

Like every parent, I have made my share of mistakes. One instance that stands out happened when Ty was just learning to read. I had him sound out several short words. He did a few but clearly found the process difficult. Still, I insisted he do one more word. He sounded out each letter successfully but could not join them in the proper order. Because we did this just before bedtime, Ty was already tired. As we continued the lesson, his fatigue won out: he became more and more frustrated, lost his concentration, and, in the end, fell apart. My insistence that he sound out this word resulted in a very angry boy going to bed in tears.

The next morning, Ty was still upset. But, by then, I was well aware of my mistake. He was not learning to read by being pushed so hard. Instead, he was learning to hate reading. I was not listening to him but heeding my own, admittedly arbitrary, schedule, just because. Why was it so important to sound out that one word? Was it to show Ty that I was boss, that I called the shots, that he had to do what I said regardless of whether it made sense or helped him? No. This could wait. Treating Ty with so little respect did not accomplish my main purpose, teaching him to read. In fact, it worked to destroy my very objective.

With these thoughts in mind, the next morning in front of all three children, I apologized to Ty. I explained why my insisting that Ty read was a mistake.

So was I a lesser parent in Ty's eyes? Had I lost his respect by admitting to being fallible? Was I to be ignored because I could not make him do as I commanded? That is, could I not expect his cooperation and obedience because he had defied me and gotten away with it? Quite the contrary, all day Ty was wonderful. He swept the sidewalk for me without being asked. Whenever I asked him to do something, he was most cooperative. And just to show he was not averse to doing schoolwork, that evening, he asked me to give him some math problems.

This same idea of giving respect and the wonderful results that ensue is an underlying message in a children's movie that was a surprise success, even among adults, a few years back. Even better than the movie is the little gem of the book upon which the movie is based. *Babe: The Gallant Pig* by Dick King-Smith is the story of a pig who learns to herd sheep. But rather than nipping their heels and terrorizing the flock as proper sheepdogs do, Babe takes a different tack. "Why," he wonders as Fly the sheepdog explains how to herd the sheep, "not just nicely ask the sheep to do what you want?" As Fly patiently explains to her novice, it is because sheep are stupid. Not much respect there.

But Babe persists on his own. The sheep, to his pleasure, respond most positively to his kind, gentle, and respectful manners. They do exactly as they are requested. Not only do they cooperate, but they do so in perfect form and ever so calmly. In the end, even Fly discovers that good manners can work wonders. However, her conversion, her respect for others, is not complete. Fly persists in believing that sheep are stupid. Babe knows better: he respects the sheep, and he is always most grateful when they do do his bidding. Not surprisingly, the sheep, in turn, respect him.

For all of us, when we give respect, the results will be most wondrous.

Chapter 4

To Trust

I eat when I am hungry,
I drink when I am dry;
If a tree don't fall on me,
I'll live 'til I die.

Understanding, respect, trust – all are necessary in successfully dealing with children. One without the others will not work. We can understand why a child acts as he does. But if we then impose our way without taking that information into account, we lack respect for him. We, in effect, tell the child he matters not.

If, instead, our understanding of the child's actions leads us to realize there are valid reasons for his behavior, we have respect for the child. We see that evil intent is not hidden behind his behavior. We see that there are logical reasons and heartfelt needs. From this understanding and respect comes trust. Respect acknowledges and accepts the individual. Trust goes beyond. It recognizes this respect based upon understanding. Further, it says we know the child's actions are based upon his needs. We believe in him; we believe he will act appropriately. With respect *for* the child, we get respect *from* the child. From this mutual respect comes mutual trust. The child trusts we will not demand from him what he is not capable of doing nor what is wrong to do. We, in turn, trust the child will behave, act appropriately, and act to satisfy his needs, not wants.

In some ways trust comes before understanding. We, in effect, say to the child, "I do not know why you are doing this. It does not seem right. But I trust that there is a good reason. I will just have to figure it out." The reasons rarely jump out at us. We often need distance in time and place, a wider perspective, or a calmer environment to evaluate what went on. Until we fully understand the child in this situation, we fall back on trust.

Of course, if we are new to this, we will likely, instead, rely on mistrust. We are still suspicious. We have to experience this revelation. We must see for ourselves that there, indeed, is meaning behind the child's action. There is reason, and we need to discover it. Then trust comes more easily.

While trust pervades our relationship with the child, it stands out during those periods of discovery. There is the gap where our understanding is lacking. We are analyzing, thinking, investigating. We do not have adequate information. We do not see the connection of seemingly unrelated actions that will give us the searched for understanding. In the meantime, our trust dominates our relationship with the child.

Chapter 5

Discipline and Respect

Here's Sulky Sue.
What shall we do?
Turn her face to the wall,
'Til she comes to.

Manners in the dining room,
Manners in the hall,
If you don't behave yourself,
You shall have none at all.

This idea – that trust and respect are built upon understanding the child – matters nowhere so much as in discipline. Or more appropriately, it is most important in fostering proper development in the child. Discipline may or may not enter the picture. Actually, the better one understands the child and the more there is mutual respect, the less discipline comes into play. Instead of disciplining, one leads or guides the child to right behavior.

Consider toddlers. Sometimes it seems all they do is create situations tailor-made for parents to practice their discipline skills. But what are they really doing? They are exploring their world. This is how they make sense of it; this is how they learn. Some may claim the toddler loves to get in trouble. But this is *our* definition of their activity. Given a cabinet, the child will explore it. First, there is the cabinet door. Open, close; open, close; open, close. We would be incredibly bored after the first round. But the child does this over and over again. He is practicing. Opening and closing doors is old hat to us; to him, it is a new experience. He is perfecting a new skill. More, he is learning that doors reveal wondrous treasures. Behind them lie all sorts of goodies. To find out exactly what, he must – you know all too well – remove every single one.

To us, this is a mess, and he is obviously getting into mischief. But wait. Consider his perspective. The child has no concept of what we call a mess – yet. A rigid sense of order will come later. For now, it is a desire for neatness that is ours and ours alone.

Second, the toddler learns through experience (as do we all). To understand his world, he must explore it physically. What he finds in the cabinet he will touch, hold, bang, mouth, lick, examine all around. He uses all of his senses – touch, hearing, sight, smell, and taste. Sometimes one sense is particularly piqued. He sees reflections in the shiny pot's surface, and they change as he moves the pot around. Or he gets a loud and very different noise when an item is dropped on the floor. Will he get the same sound when he drops it again? There is only one way to find out: do it again. He is a little scientist constantly coming upon new worlds, devising new theories, and testing his hunches. The only trouble is that Mom and Dad do not share his perspective.

Chastising the child for doing what is both natural and necessary for proper growth is counterproductive. The child needs to figure out his world. He needs to understand it. He needs to physically encounter it. This does not mean we tolerate his exploration and destruction of everything in his path. Instead, it means we create an environment where his investigations will hurt neither him nor others nor prized possessions. We remove dangerous substances, precious objects are placed out of reach, and certain cabinets are childproofed. But always, we keep available some items and places where exploration is safe. If much time is spent in the kitchen, at least one cabinet has pots and pans that can be played with. Periodically, we vary the items in it so the contents will continue to appeal to the child.

The same goes for other areas of the house. In each room in which the child spends much time, we have something he can explore without requiring a hovering parent. It can be a closet or bottom drawer or even just a cardboard box of toys.

The outdoors has even greater appeal for our budding scientists. There is so much that sparks their curiosity. Often what is boring and overlooked by us will intrigue them for hours. Although hardly a toddler, Ty, when he was about seven, spent hours a day over the course of weeks just watching ants in our front yard.

Such fascinations are why hikes or walks with young children often do not go well. It is not necessarily that they lack the strength or stamina to walk the distance. It is more that their interest lies not in reaching the destination or in taking in the views. These are adult reasons for this activity. Instead, children are interested in their immediate, close-up surroundings. They want to squat, look, and ponder what they see right there before them: the bugs, the hollowed out tree, the stream.

To keep a young one entertained for a while, all one needs is dirt, water, and accepting parents. I watched with amusement two different families dealing with the first two ingredients for kiddie fun, but without the last. It had recently rained, so inviting puddles were abundant. A father ran to stop his toddler from running through a puddle. Having swooped up the child, a slightly older sibling then headed for the same attraction. The father had his hands full juggling children and keeping them dry. A few yards beyond, a mother was doing her best to keep her own youngster from splashing in the puddles.

So what is the big deal? Why must children stay neat, clean, and dry? With the modern convenience of washing machines, dirty clothes are readily taken care of. Both of these families were at a park, visiting the children's playground. It is not a place where one remains clean but where children are expected to indulge in messy play. Children love to feel – with their bodies, their hands, their feet. If rubber boots are not at hand, remove socks and shoes. It is fine at the beach; why not also on the sidewalk or at the park? We adults prefer to stay dry and clean. But our preferences are at odds with those of most children. Worse, what we want goes against what children need.

✓ Children need to explore their world directly. They need physical contact with it. And they need to have fun doing it. There will be time enough in their lives for cleanliness, as we adults well know. For now, they need their adults to understand their need to explore. In a nutshell, letting the child explore his world is more important than keeping clothes clean and dry. If the parent cannot bear to let some items get dirty, she can keep some old ones ready for outdoor explorations.

We must be careful about projecting our own responses to the world onto our children. If *we* were to get wet, we might very well feel chilled. That is not necessarily so for our child. I watched in amazement as our seven-year-old friend played in the cold waters of Puget Sound. The water temperature could not have been more than 55°. To have merely gotten my feet wet would have been chilling to me. Yet here was this boy romping in and out of the water. And he was warm. He felt so both to himself and to anyone who touched his skin.

Understanding the child makes disciplining so much easier. If we, for instance, understand that our feeling of cold is not necessarily also our child's feeling, there will be far fewer battles over the clothing he must wear. Instead, the child will dress according to his response to the weather. Of course, if he is dressing in line with the inside house "weather," he may have to feel the outside to figure out what other items he needs to put on. Rarely have my walking children needed as much bundling as I give myself. Their needs are different. Most often, it is because they are more active. In just walking, they take several steps for each one of ours. And walking is rarely the favored mode of movement. Running or jumping is much more fun. All of this means that these little ones will generate far more heat in their bodies than will their slowly walking parents.

This is not to say that we parents go unprepared. On extended forays in the outdoors, we prudent parents naturally take along extra clothing for the child because we, as the older, wiser, and more experienced adults, realize that the weather may change or the child at rest may cool down. What we want to avoid is bundling up now for conditions the child will react to only much later.

Just as there will be times when the child will need extra clothing, so, too, there will be times when puddles will be off limits. Understanding works both ways. Having been allowed to indulge in puddle jumping because his needs are understood, the child will be more accepting of the rare times when such play is off limits. It is the child's turn to understand, for instance, that puddle splashing is not allowed when dressed for going to a party or the theater.

Invariably, there will be times when discipline will be needed. I suspect even in an ideal world, children would challenge authority if for no other reason than to test the limits. Are they truly boundaries for them? Do the parents (teachers, neighbors, store clerks) really mean it? And, even if so, what are the consequences?

I have found that when transgressions are made, if the consequences are reasonable for the situation, everyone feels good.

When I was little, my siblings and I got into our share of trouble. Being in a relatively rural area with few neighbor children, this trouble invariably involved altercations with each other. I have no recollection of our at-home mother disciplining us, although I am sure she did. What do stand out in my memory are the consequences. When our father arrived home from work in the evening, he would be told of our many misdeeds. Whacks to our bottoms would result, usually with time alone in our bedrooms added for emphasis. The punishments were out of line with our misbehavior. There was simply no connection. They took place long after whatever it was we had done. They were unrelated to the specifics of the case – always whacks regardless of different transgressions. And they did nothing to change our behavior. No one felt better for the experience: we spanked children certainly did not feel good, and I suspect my father did not really enjoy playing the heavy.

In contrast, when my children have misbehaved and have experienced reasonable or natural consequences, we all do feel better.

At one point, both of my daughters were averse to brushing their teeth in the morning. At night, it was no problem. It was part of their nightly routine, and they followed it faithfully. The morning routine was another matter altogether. I suspect this was partly due to it needing to be done soon after breakfast. Since breakfast and the anticipations and actuality of a new, wonder-filled day had energized the girls, the last thing they wanted to do was something as mundane and still and quiet as brushing teeth in a little room. Instead, they wanted to run around or play outside. In retrospect, it probably would have been best to have let them play for a while – half an hour or so – and then done tooth brushing. But I suspected that this requirement would have been forgotten by me as well as the children as we all became focused on the day's activities.

Instead, I tried various methods, but none seemed to work. In desperation, after once again having to remind the girls umpteen times to brush their teeth, I grounded them for a week. Later that day, I reflected on my action. I realized I had been in a rotten mood when I had meted out that edict; I had overreacted. A week's grounding was extreme in length. It was inappropriate in application. At their ages, grounding had little impact as they both spent tremendous amounts of time playing at home on their own anyway.

As part of my looking at the situation afresh, I consulted the girls. What should I do, I asked them, so they would brush their teeth without my constant reminders? Each came up with a different idea. Rikki, the younger one, said she should not be allowed to play with her best buddy for two days. Her older sister, Rhiannon, said she should not be allowed to read any books for two days. (I suppose some may think that this was a ploy on her part to have the equivalent of no punishment. But, no, Rhiannon spent many hours each day reading; so, indeed, to be denied that would be a true punishment.) Fine, we all agreed.

The next morning, Rikki did not brush her teeth, so I imposed her chosen punishment: no playing with her best friend for two days. As this was a weekend, it was a particularly harsh punishment. Her friend was close-by, so this was two full days – not just afternoons – of no play.

The result was that Rikki was especially nice, going out of her way to help everyone without even being asked. She also spent quite a bit of time close to me. I am not sure if this was her way of asking forgiveness. It may have been, but because she seemed so happy in what she was doing, she likely had a simpler reason behind her behavior and mood. I believe she just felt good: she had done something wrong and now was living with what she had chosen as a consequence.

While my children have had their share of misdeeds, they have not always chosen the punishments. Choice by them is not nearly as important as sensing that what results is fair and consistent.

Another time, Rikki went against several rules of the house. She went to a friend's house not to play but just to watch TV. (My children are allowed to watch TV only on special occasions, such as sleepovers.) She had a high-sugar snack at a neighbor's even though healthful alternatives were at home. And she had food just before dinnertime even after being told not to. In all cases, Rikki was open about her transgressions. In the first two, she even volunteered the information: "Mom, do you promise not to get angry if I tell you something?" So I did not get angry, but I did punish her. Afterwards she was all love.

A parent could go crazy trying to understand every little action of the child. In the above case, I never really knew why Rikki did what she did. She could have been testing the rules. She could have been tempted by the treats others are allowed to have. She could have been yearning for more attention from me. I will never know. In this situation, it is not all that important. These were isolated incidents. She did not spend days at friends' houses wasting her time in front of the television or filling up on sugar whenever she got the chance. She did wrong; she knew it; she was punished. Then it was over; only love remained.

The understanding that is needed here is not for the meaning of every little, individual action. They are too minor to bother with. And, in some ways, it would be too intrusive otherwise. The child needs to have some degree of privacy. It is unfair to be constantly analyzing the child's every move. We parents have plenty to do as it is!

Where the understanding comes into play here is in the response. The child needs to know that the rules do apply. There is security in having some sort of boundary and in having parents who are consistent rather than arbitrary or not caring. Having rules lets the child know there are limits. Enforcing the rules shows the child that the parents mean what they say; they are believable and trustworthy. This invariably carries over to other areas. Giving one's word has significance whether it is "This is the rule; obey it" or "I said I will spend this evening playing with you, and I will." Enforcing the rules also shows that the parent cares. It takes effort to be involved. It risks being seen as the "meanie" who punishes. But the caring parent does not shirk this role.

Had Rikki consistently violated one or more rules, a totally different approach would have been taken. Then an attempt at understanding her actions would have been made. Among questions asked would have been "Am I, the parent, being too harsh?" or "Can the rules be relaxed and still be in line with good child-rearing practices?" Questions would have revolved around not only possible reasons on Rikki's part but also on her parents' parts. What part had we or other adults played in this?

I had another time when all three children were seemingly crying for discipline. This time, it was Rhiannon who was caught watching TV at a friend's house. Unlike the incident with Rikki, this one had been going on for some time. Nor did Rhiannon appear to feel any guilt in going against our rules. There was shame in being caught, perhaps, but not guilt for her behavior. On the same day that I discovered this about Rhiannon, Rikki had removed a next-door neighbor's loose fence board and sawn it up for her own use. Ty had also gone to town with the handsaw. Some time before, I had told him he could remove any branches on a lilac bush that had no leaves since those branches were dead. That was summer. It was now late fall and he had found many more leafless branches. Unfortunately, most of them had been alive. Not satisfied with that sawing opportunity, he had moved on to our, admittedly, rickety Adirondack chair. Its sad shape was now sadder thanks to several saw marks in its arms.

All three knew they had done wrong; all were appropriately punished. The saw enthusiasts lost saw privileges for a week. Rhiannon's case was a different matter. Since Rhiannon had continually disobeyed, she was barred from her friend's house for a month.

As this was not an isolated incident for Rhiannon, I had to go through those questions suggested previously. Was this "no television" rule too extreme? Was I somehow to blame? Was more going on than what was most obvious? After much thought, I concluded "no" to all three. After being in school all day, Rhiannon's friend wanted only to "veg" out in front of the television. After being with siblings all day, Rhiannon wanted only to be with others, even if doing so meant defying the rules. While relaxing the rules would allow Rhiannon to have time with her friend, it would not provide meaningful time. If television viewing was all the two girls could think of doing together, the friendship rested on shaky ground. Even when done in the company of others, watching television is still a solitary, passive experience. My reasons for eliminating television from my children's lives remained. Nor did it make sense to forbid television at home but allow viewing at others' homes. So the rules remained. And if the rules were more likely to be broken when with a certain friend, then that friend would be off-limits. In this case, the restriction would be for a month.

Those transgressions, even Rhiannon's repeated defiance of the television rules, did not make the children untrustworthy. A few days later when a neighbor asked me to visit for a few hours in the evening, I accepted. The three children were left by themselves. (Although the oldest was 11, she was never put in charge of the others. I always expected each to be in charge of him- or herself.) After about an hour and a half, Rhiannon called to ask when I was coming home. I said my good-byes and returned home to find all three children with pajamas on, with teeth brushed, and on the couch waiting for their bedtime story.

Understanding our child means also understanding children in general. One bad act does not make a bad child. One transgression does not mean others will follow. We must remember children are learning. Not only do they need to have limits and have those limits enforced. They also need help in learning how to remain within those boundaries. For Rhiannon, the temptation of the forbidden television was too much, especially since her friend did not have the same restriction. Any friend who assists in rule breaking is not a friend to spend time with. Rhiannon's month-long separation from her friend reinforced this. It also gave her lots of opportunity to figure out how to make good use of her time in ways other than watching television.

For Rikki, I suspect, the need for a certain piece of wood was too great to resist a board that was barely in place and did not matter enough to the neighbors to fix. Rikki obviously needed help in learning to respect other people's property, regardless of one's own needs – or, rather, wants. Ty's lesson was much the same. Sawing is fun, but one does not indiscriminately saw on whatever catches one's fancy.

As much as I may have understood why the children did as they did, that knowledge did not excuse them. They are still the ones responsible for their actions. Even if Rhiannon's friend invited her in to watch television knowing full well that Rhiannon was not allowed to do so, it was still Rhiannon who acted upon her own decision. No one forced Rikki's or Ty's hands on the saw. They did it and chose to do it.

This seems quite natural: one is responsible for one's action. Yet not all would agree.

Ty was playing with another boy, a few years older and bigger. They were roughhousing, and Ty's head hit a hard object. After comforting Ty, I told the boy that that was enough; there would be no more rough playing. His older sister rushed to the rescue, saying it was not her brother's fault because he was not used to playing with younger or smaller children.

Excuse me! So whose fault is it? I probably would not have been involved had the boy showed any remorse or, at least, concern about the results of his action. Instead, his stance was the same as his sister's: it was not his fault. In effect, this says that at ten years of age, the boy was not yet in control of his body. He just lashed out wildly without regard to the specific situation. There was no concept of whether he was at play or in serious self-defense, whether he was wrestling with one weaker or one stronger or an equal. Worse, he was not willing to learn how to be gentler. He never said anything to indicate that he was sorry and would be more careful next time. In fact, given what he did say, it was apparent that the scene would likely be repeated, as he had no desire to change his ways. Further, he would likely continue to defend himself as he continued to hurt once again.

Children do not normally behave so. Certainly, bullies or those filled with anger will purposely hurt others, especially the easy targets, those weaker than they. But normal children do not. When quite young, they respond with empathy to another's pain. Whether or not they have inflicted the pain, they will show concern toward the other. Even infants upon hearing another one cry will join in.

Certainly, having physical interaction with other children allows children to learn the effects of their actions. And continued play enables them to learn to adapt, to be less rough and more controlled, if mistakes in judgment have been made. But the child does not need other children for this. Adults, especially parents, can help him learn.

A time-honored way of doing that is in roughhousing with Dad. My daughters as well as my son relished such play. For them, a night was not complete without a long roughhousing session with their dad. But, always, Keith kept the play under control.

Little girls and boys alike take pleasure in such close interaction with their dads. Being aware of his strength, the father controls himself so he does not hurt the child. He keeps the game fun by letting the child get the upper hand once in a while. But he remains aware of how the child is responding to the situation. Inevitably, the child will tire. It is hard for a young child to stop such play when it is so much fun, even if he is exhausted. Or the child may get frustrated and then lose his self-control. That is when the parent ends the game. Or the especially sensitive parent ends it just before that point. Then the parent, by example, shows how control is maintained so no one gets hurt. The parent controls his actions during play, and he limits the playtime when it may get out of hand.

We show that limits are not just arbitrary. There is a reason for them, a benefit for the child. The limit may be time-dependent. So the father may roughhouse only for so long. Even though it is fun and the child wants to continue, the time constraint ensures all ends happily.

The limit may be physical. So roughhousing is done only in certain places, such as on carpeted floors with no furniture nearby. Even though roughhousing is so much fun that the child wants it anywhere, the physical limits ensure play is safe and no one gets hurt.

The limit may be more nebulous and not so easily defined. So the father ends roughhousing as the child begins to lose control and has obviously tired. This also ensures the experience is a pleasant one for all.

This is where the child trusts the parent. Through the mutual understanding, respect, and trust that the parent and child have established over many instances of being together, the child knows these are cases where his parent is to be trusted. The parent knows best when to stop. Likely, too, there will be times when the timing is off, and the child discovers firsthand what happens when play continues too long.

So both parent and child learn to distinguish between limits that are firm (such as no playing in the street) and those that may be challenged (such as bedtime on a weekend night).

The parent also responds appropriately when hurt. He is not angry but is providing information. He is reminding the child to be aware of what he is doing and how that affects the other. Behind all of this is the idea of having fun. And it is fun for both only as long as no one gets hurt.

This is not learned in only one game, but over time in many sessions. And because it is fun whether with another child or an adult, the child tries to prolong it. Again, that can happen if no one gets hurt. But even if one is hurt, play can continue. If apologies are sincerely given and the damage is not severe, the wrestling or roughhousing often goes on. What is present is awareness of the effect of one's own actions, of one's own strength in relation to the other's, of fatigue of one or the other. What embraces all of this is mutual respect. That is, those playing are doing it for fun and not to hurt the other.

Lacking in Ty's session with the boy was awareness and control based upon that awareness. That fun was the main intent was not evident in the other boy. He may very well have not been used to playing with a smaller child. But since he *knew* Ty was smaller and weaker, as both he and his sister indicated, he should have altered his action. Instead, it seemed he felt that excuse was permission to act irresponsibly and without restraint.

Chapter 6

Discipline and Disrespect

What are little boys made of, made of?
What are little boys made of?
Frogs and snails
And puppy-dog tails,
That's what little boys are made of.

James Gilligan is a professor of psychiatry at Harvard Medical School. Through his practice, he has contact with prisoners. A revealing point for him occurred when a prisoner that guards could no longer control was brought to him. Gilligan asked what the man wanted most of all. "Pride. Dignity. Self-esteem" was his reply.

This is no less true for our children. If we want their cooperation and their respect, we must first give them our respect.

Oscar Wilde was right about the parents of his age as well as about those of our own time. He said, "Few parents nowadays pay any respect to what their children say to them. The old-fashioned respect for the young is fast dying out."

I think, too often, we adults are just not aware of what we are doing to our children. Our intentions are good – to get them to behave respectfully, to obey us, to listen to us, to learn from us. But how we go about it often falls far short of the mark.

For instance, it is quite common and certainly reasonable for parents to expect their children not to interrupt them when they are in conversation with another person. I have seen such polite children come up to their parents and wait with more patience than any adult would ever show. Almost oblivious to the child, the parent talks on. Should another adult join the group, accommodations are made. Meanwhile, the child waits on and on and on. It takes mere seconds to pause in the conversation and ask the child what is wanted and then respond. Instead, the all-important adult conversation is carried to conclusion.

The poor child. Is that how an adult would be treated – basically ignored? I know that is not so, for adults not part of the group *are* acknowledged and given the opportunity to speak up. Why not a child?

The obvious message is that the child is less important.

I was raised during the time when children were expected to be seen but not heard. This says, in effect, "Children do not disturb us; we want to have our own quiet conversation." This is a different message than the above. That says, "Come if you have a question, but wait until I acknowledge you." Since that acknowledgement may not come, this message is a dishonest one. Having been part of many adult gatherings where children have waited for acknowledgement, I know that the conversations never interrupted are not so important that pause could not be taken for the child. Instead, the whole scenario tells the child that he matters little.

There is another equally common display of this attitude toward children. It is an annual ritual that clearly says children do not count. Modern-day Halloween is a time for children to dress up in costumes and walk the neighborhood while gathering as much candy as possible. Upon their return home, the children examine their booty: the goods are dumped, counted, and sorted. And, of course, a few or maybe more are eaten. This is too much for many parents to bear. The temptation of such vast amounts of candy cannot be resisted. The more polite parents ask their children for some candy. Those less respectful demand some. Then there are those who simply take it. Once a neighbor friend stashed his candy in our house to keep his father and siblings from raiding his store of candy. Even then, there was some trepidation in the arrangement since he was not used to trusting his family; why would ours be any different?

Regardless of whether the parents ask, demand, or just take, the implication is the same. The parents, as the all-powerful ones, get their way. Some of the candy must be surrendered. Even the pseudo-polite request for candy is a veiled demand. The option to refuse is not really there.

Parents who do this justify it in many ways. For some, it is the fact that there is an overwhelming excess of sweets. They might say that because the child has so much, the candy should be shared. In reality, it is because the parent sees so much and cannot resist having some. The logical extension of this reasoning is to take from anyone who has more than we do. In our society this is called "stealing."

What kind of an example are parents setting? Think from the child's perspective. The child is not learning to share by being forced to give up what he has. Instead, he is learning that the powerful ones make the decisions. They can say and do whatever they want. They can take whatever candy they want from their own child.

Why does society rule against taking from others but let the same practice pass when it is a parent taking from the powerless child? It is simply that too few parents truly respect their children. A law-abiding adult would no more grab a friend's bounty than take from a stranger. Yet he will not think twice to do so to his own child.

Most children I know whose parents take their trick-or-treat candy to eat just accept this state of affairs. They do not like it. They know it is disrespectful. Yet they also know that they have no choice.

Some parents take the candy not to eat it themselves but to regulate the child's consumption of sweets. That is an entirely different matter. It is still the child's candy; it is still only the child who eats it. This practice respects the child and understands him. It recognizes that the candy is the child's. But it also recognizes that the child does not yet have sufficient self-control to keep from overindulging in sweets.

Sometimes this disrespect is harder to discern because it is masked by good intentions, such as forcing children to give to others. We believe that by making them perform charitable acts they will then want to do them on their own. It is not so simple.

During one of my visits to a classroom of nine- to twelve-year-olds, I found the children involved in making ornaments for people in a nursing home. The teacher had chosen the project, and the students had agreed to it. As I listened to the students during their work, it became apparent that they did not really wish to give their ornaments to the nursing home residents. This was the teacher's idea. He felt, like the parents who see their children's mounds of candy at Halloween, that the children all had so much that they should be willing to share. He felt, also, that since they had agreed to do the project, they should follow through.

But there were several problems with his interpretation. First, when a teacher suggests a child do something, the suggestion is rarely one where the child has a choice. It is a command, similar to that given when parents "ask" their children for Halloween candy. The children's agreement is an empty commitment since they feel they really have no choice.

Second, the children were not selfish. Instead, because they were putting so much time into these ornaments, they very much wished to share. But they wanted to give them to people whom they cared about – their parents or other relatives. The residents of the nursing home were strangers to them. There was no meaningful relationship between them nor would there be, as this was a one-time contact with these senior citizens.

Finally, children do not learn to give from the heart by being forced to give. There is no meaning for them in such acts. Instead, they are merely following orders. In such instances, there is no commitment. They are doing what another has said they "should" do. The act is not internalized; it has no lasting effect. It stops once the person saying the child should give is no longer around. When the external impetus is gone, the reason for so doing also goes.

Putting such demands upon children shows no respect for them. It says their feelings about giving and their choices of recipients carry no weight. It says that only the adult should decide here. This is hardly the way to get cooperation from the child, by imposing our way and ignoring his.

Had these school children been allowed to make their ornaments and do with them as they chose, a far better lesson would have been learned. They would have realized the joy in sharing something one values with someone one loves. The pleasure in giving would be remembered. It is only a few steps further to see that giving to anyone can be pleasurable, as long as the giver is in control of giving – what to give, to whom to give, when to give. Remove that control and place it in the adults' hands, and we get what I saw in these children: resentment and far from charitable feeling for the eventual recipients.

Such instances of adults denying respect for children extends beyond the holidays. It enters into the most mundane of circumstances. Look at what happens in our homes on a regular basis.

It takes considerable time and effort to run a household. In families where both parents work full-time, it is especially difficult to squeeze all chores in the off-work hours and still have some personal free time. It is only natural to expect children to share in the work. This is true even if the parents are not both employed outside the home. It reinforces the idea that all members of a household contribute to it according to their capabilities.

What is disrespectful is not the assigning of chores per se, but the way in which it is done. For example, when we got our puppy, everyone was ready to help out. That meant exercising the dog, feeding him, and scooping up and disposing of his mess. The three children, who had all wanted a dog, had no problem with this shared responsibility. They had had pets before and knew that work and fun were both parts of having an animal.

This was all well and good until their father told them they should scoop up after the dog for him. Everyone had assigned days to be totally responsible for the dog. Their dad was saying, in effect, that he wished to partake only of the pleasurable aspects of dog care on his days. The distasteful parts were to be shunted off to the children. The unfairness of the situation did not escape the children. Howls of protest and refereeing by Mom reestablished fairness for all.

Yet the damage had been done. The children knew their dad saw them as easy targets for his share of unpleasant work. There was no acknowledgement on his part of the fact that they were doing their share – and that most willingly. And worst of all, he was setting a most unfortunate example to his children. He was showing that the parent can make unjust rules merely by virtue of his power. Rather than considering what is fair for all, the all-powerful one can, instead, just rule in his favor.

Parents and adults in general expect respect from children. This is as it should be. Because of their vaster experience and, one would hope, greater wisdom, adults should be looked up to. This position is abused, however, when it is used to bully children into working for them.

Again, it is not the work itself that is onerous. In any situation, all family members can be expected to contribute effort according to their ability. In addition, it is expected that younger members of society show deference to their elders. So, for instance, when public seating is scarce, youths should give up their seats for the elderly; young adults would, of course, do the same.

This deference does not, however, equate to servitude. Many times, I have seen parents, comfortably seated and doing little other than reading or watching television, order their children about. More often than not, the children are fully engaged in an activity where disruption is not appreciated. So the child must extract himself and get the drink for the parent or answer the phone that is invariably for the parent or retrieve the magazine as requested.

This does not teach the child to respect the parent. Instead, the child learns to resent being ordered about. The parent is fully capable of getting what is desired. It is only laziness and an abuse of power that enables him to take advantage of the child. One does not learn to respect another by being taken advantage of. One learns respect by being respected.

In contrast, I have seen children without prompting serve the elderly. They will ask how they can help, if the elder would like something to drink, and what they can do to make him or her more comfortable. In these actions, the children demonstrate their respect for the older ones. In this way, they acknowledge that the older ones need special care and even have earned the right to be catered to. At the same time, the older ones are receptive to such deference, seeing it not as an insult to their perceived lack of capability but as a recognition of their place of honor due to their years of living.

While I do not yet consider myself among such older ones, my children do treat me with respect. When I need help, I ask and receive it. Help is immediate because the children know I ask only when truly needed. I will do my part and never ask for assistance out of laziness. At the same time, when circumstances call for extra effort, all chip in. For instance, when company is expected, everyone, without being asked, helps clean up. There is the recognition that all will benefit from the visitors, so all work to prepare for their coming. I respect the children as much as they do me.

Of course, respect in the form of helping out is not limited to such instances. We also do favors for one another just out of niceness. So one is allowed to be lazy, so to speak, as another pours the milk for everyone else. This, too, is a reflection of mutual respect. One does not think, "I will do for you so that you will owe me one." Instead, one recognizes that the other's attitude is generous, open, and respectful to him so his actions reflect this.

One of the most memorable examples of this mutual respect came to me in high school. As is the case even today in most schools, we students were expected to address our teachers with a title. So it was "Mr. Smith" or "Mrs. Jones." ("Ms." was unheard of then.) We students were, of course, called by our first names or sometimes our full names. There was one exception. My freshman biology teacher, Mr. Gromme, addressed us students by title, so for me it was "Miss Moss." It was odd at first. The more common means of calling students gave emphasis to the belief that the titled person, the teacher, was more important and in control; the untitled person, the student, was subservient. Certainly, we students did have much to learn from our teachers. Yet Mr. Gromme addressing us as we did him did not negate this. Instead, we felt respected. We sensed a recognition by this teacher that we could attain his level of learning (eventually), that our minds were as capable as his (with some guidance), that his classroom was where serious learning took place. We did not lose respect for him because he placed us on a level with him through this simple form of address. Certainly, he raised us to his level. But to be placed on his level meant there were high – adult – expectations of us. Indeed, there was no goofing off in class. As he respected us, so did we, him.

For mutual respect to work, it must first be given. And who gives respect first? Are not we parents the leaders? Leaders do. And leaders go first. Leaders do not wait for others. Respect comes first from us to the child. By example, the child learns.

This concept of giving respect before receiving it is in contrast to those who rule by fear. For them, respect is a one-way street. It only comes to them from the child; it does not go to the child from the adult. It is far easier to use one's power as parent to instill fear in the child and thus gain obedience. After all, it works. Or it usually does. Or it seems to. Some children will rebel against the treatment that invariably results from fear-based parenting. Some will refuse to cry out when struck in punishment. Some will run away. Some will only mentally retreat, their bodies being hurt while their minds wander into a safe area.

Whatever the method, the idea is the same. The child is attempting to retain some semblance of dignity, of self-respect. It goes back to Gilligan's study of prisoners who he found were hungry for others to recognize their worthiness. When the parents, teachers, and other adults react to the child by trying to instill fear, they are denying respect. The child has no dignity who is ruled by fear.

And what does the child learn? It depends. Some children learn by example. As they are treated, so will they treat others. When the adults in their lives deny them their dignity, this denial does not take away their need for it. They still hunger for it. They try to regain it in whatever way they can. For such children, the way to get this respect is to do what the adults have shown them to do. They have been taught all too well. They use their position of relative power to instill fear in those they can, those younger, smaller, or weaker than they.

Fortunately, not all learn the same lesson. Some see what is done and refuse to carry it on. They realize such treatment is not right. They remember the pain, and, rather than meting it out to others, they use this remembrance to keep from giving others the same pain. They do not grow up to repeat the mistakes of the adults in their lives. Instead, they use the example for knowing what *not* to do to others. Not all those who were abused as children become child abusers. Many rise above their experiences.

Sadly, not all learn the lesson in that way. Some are beaten sufficiently into submission so as to lose all spirit. There is no desire to dominate others. But there is no desire for anything at all. The child is like a beaten horse, having no spirit, no life, no will to do anything lest it be the wrong thing.

The analogy to a beaten horse is, indeed, appropriate. A horse that is "broken in" is taught to be saddled and ridden by force, sometimes even by beatings. It is a far different horse from one that is taught by "gentling." Monty Roberts (author of *The Man Who Listens to Horses*) is one of the great promoters of gentling horses. He has experienced both methods of training horses. His father broke horses and could not accept any other way of teaching horses to obey. Like authoritarian parents, he felt that one had to have the upper hand through fear. If the horse did not fear the rider or trainer, it would not obey. Although he expected his son to train horses in the same tried and true way, his son discovered a better method. Through extensive studies of horses in the wild, Monty Roberts learned how horses communicate with each other. He did what is suggested over and over again in our study of children. He simply watched. Roberts went to where the wild mustangs run free and just observed them. For hours and hours, for days at a time, and always unobtrusively, he lay or sat on the range and watched the horses. Over time, what the horses did began to make sense to him. Their behavior was not random, not chaotic, not senseless. He saw that there was a connection between what one horse did to another and the subsequent behavior of that other horse. He saw how the mares taught their young to obey with specific movements of the body. Certain positions were warnings, others were threats, and some were even apologies. So, too, was there similar communication among the stallions and others in the herd.

Put another way, Roberts understood horses. Through his understanding, he developed methods to gentle a horse. That is, he got the horse's permission to accept bridle, saddle, and rider. Such a horse retains its spirit, its dignity, if you will. Such a horse works with its rider, just as the rider works with the horse. They are a unit, working together, and, yes, respecting each other.

Significantly, Roberts' father raised his son as he raised horses, by breaking him in. Just as significantly, Monty Roberts recognized in the methods for gentling horses those methods that work best with children. The legacy of father beating son and son growing up to repeat the pattern ended with Roberts' father. Respect was the key that the younger Roberts discovered. Whether dealing with horses or people or any other creature, treating the other with respect is the only way to work together.

This idea of respect pervades all in our life. In the introduction to *The Singing Creek Where the Willows Grow* by Opal Whiteley, Benjamin Hoff describes Opal's relationship to her natural world. She was on an intimate level with it and made incredible discoveries for one so young. In fact, when she was seventeen and without a high school diploma, she approached the University of Oregon in Eugene. The head of the university's geology department stated that she knew more about geology than did graduates of his department. The head of the botany department wondered if studying in school was actually a waste of time if, as Opal demonstrated, one could learn so much on her own.

How did Opal learn so much without an instructor or books to guide her? It was not only by being in the woods. Just as for Monty Roberts, his understanding of horses came not merely from watching the mustangs. After all, many people spend hours in the forests or with horses, but their level of knowing is not nearly as extensive. As Benjamin Hoff says of what Opal accomplished, "... the natural world has a great deal to teach inquirers who approach it with respect. But only incomplete answers will be obtained by those who try to force its secrets from it."

So, too, is it with our children. Certainly, we must be around our children to allow understanding to even happen. But that is not sufficient. Our attitude affects what we see as well as what happens in our presence. With respect for the child, a world previously hidden opens up to us. Only then is understanding possible.

A child treated with respect is like Roberts' horses or Opal's forests. The individual spirit lives. The essence of the being flourishes. Such a child works *with* the adult. The two are as a unit, cooperative and working toward the same goal. It is like my children when guests are expected. We all work together to prepare. There is no need to order anyone. There is no rebelling or even delaying. All know what must be done, and it is done.

This is not an unattainable ideal. We all can do it. Time and again, I have seen the wonders unfold when children are respected. Sadly, I have seen the tragic results when that respect is withdrawn. Most vivid in my memory is what happened in a classroom years ago.

When my children were young, I taught art in the children's school. On this day, the teacher was absent, and the class had a substitute. Because it was a Montessori school where class work is highly individualized, the substitute was content just to oversee the children. There was no way she could step in and direct the students, each of whom was at a different point in each subject matter. In effect, the class was very relaxed.

My art class fit in well with this. Since Halloween was approaching, the holiday was the inspiration for our work. I had a list of several projects from which each student could choose. Some were rather mundane, such as cutting and gluing colored paper to make a paper chain for the classroom. Others were more complex and even required some scientific study, such as drawing, cutting out, and assembling an accurate human skeleton.

Regardless of the project chosen, all of the children launched into it with enthusiasm. I had always run my art lessons with the stipulation that only those who wanted to participate could. Usually, some declined the opportunity. This time, all were participating. Much was accomplished in the short time I was allotted, and completed projects were hung up.

The impact of this exercise was far greater than what was seen in the displays in the classroom. Until this time, the class had had its share of problems. Certain individuals were shunned or mistreated by others. Some students were always down on themselves or moped (not just during my art lessons!). Because the class size was small, these social and psychological problems significantly affected the workings of the whole class.

During this art session where individual desires were met, the students flourished. Those who normally were at each others' throats were working contentedly together. This cooperation carried over into lunchtime and recess. It was the first time in my many months of visits where I saw the students working as a unit even while working independently.

Unfortunately, the positive effects were short-lived. This was not because respecting the child has short-term benefits, but because adults are often shortsighted.

One week later when I returned for the next art lesson, I expected to see a class decked out in all its Halloween trappings. Instead, I was surprised to see absolutely nothing. When the children told me what had happened, I was devastated although not nearly as much as they likely had been.

The school director had felt that the children were spending too much time on the project. But rather than have it put aside or worked on in free time, she tore everything down and destroyed it.

Here was work the children had put much time and effort into. They had done so willingly and joyfully. That they felt respected in doing it had showed in how they then treated each other, also respectfully.

Now their work was gone. It was a tremendous demonstration of disrespect, saying with action as well as word that their work was nothing, a waste, not fit for display. It was a slap in the face, and the children reacted as would be expected. The respect for others that had been in place the week before lay in a heap with the decorations: it was all gone. Actually, the workings of the class were worse than ever. Frustration and anger over the director's action still seethed within the children and came out in interactions with fellow classmates.

To give respect and then take it away is far worse than not having given it in the first place. In finally getting respect, one realizes what has been missing. Take it then away, and a gaping hole remains. One now knows what is needed to fill it, but there is nothing.

The director in all likelihood felt she was doing the right thing. The children were in school and should be working on academic subjects. So remove the distraction, and they can once again concentrate on the academic.

The shortsightedness of this approach is unfortunate. Had the director allowed the children to continue – or at least leave up what was on display – their self-respect would have remained. (Imagine how far just a verbal recognition of their efforts would have gone.) With self-respect intact, the academic work of the classroom would have progressed more smoothly. As it was, all of the psychological problems of before resurfaced and continued to interfere with class work. In outward appearances, it was a well-functioning class with children working on their academic subjects. But a closer look would reveal that the class was not functioning so well. While bodies were at the books, minds were not. They were thinking instead of what another had just said or done to them, of what they would do in retaliation, of what others thought of them. It was only a matter of time – recess, lunchtime, a break to sharpen a pencil – before those thoughts became action.

Unfortunately, this is not an isolated incident of the incredible disrespect adults in this country give to children. One has only to travel in a foreign country to see the contrast in attitudes toward children. Children are treated as special. Even parents with young children are given special privileges. For instance, in long lines, such families are allowed to "skip" ahead. This is not law. It is the result of common understanding that little children easily grow tired of long waits in lines. It is in deference to them that the others in line let the young ones with their parents go before them. So, too, in restaurants children are doted upon by the staff. They know it is hard for little ones to wait for food when hungry. So tidbits are brought to ease the wait for the main course. One need not even travel abroad to experience such attention. We saw it given to our children when they were little and we ate in ethnic restaurants staffed by those still connected to their native cultures.

Contrast such attitudes to what typically happens in our country. Families with small children are seated in isolated areas of a restaurant. Eyes roll if young children are assigned airline seats near adults. Children are a bother. They are trouble and noise and a distraction. Rather than understanding, as do people of many foreign cultures, that little children tire easily, get irritable when hungry, have narrow ear canals that painfully swell on airplanes, etc., American adults ignore children's special needs. Rather than realizing children are different, American adults expect children to behave as adults do. Rather than accommodating little children based on understanding their special needs, American adults turn their backs on them in disgust because the children act just like, well, just like children.

Disrespect for children enters into the most innocuous aspects of life. It is as if the commonly held belief is that children just do not matter. For instance, according to Clifford Stoll in *Silicon Snake Oil: Second Thoughts on the Information Highway,* many children's software does not let children save their work. The message is clear. Because it is merely children's work, it is not worth keeping. Only adult work is valuable and worth retaining. Work is evaluated only in terms of adult capabilities rather than relative to the one who has done it.

This point was illustrated in a story I heard years ago. After a parent-teacher conference, a parent came home with an armful of work done by her child. On her way into the house and in view of her child, she dumped all into the trashcan. Naturally, the poor child was devastated.

That story was told to me by a teacher. He was warning me to make sure my child did not see me throw out her schoolwork that I got from our parent-teacher conference. That is, it is all right to throw out children's work without asking them. Just make sure they do not see us doing it.

This same disregard for children's work was demonstrated in my daughters' preschool. When she was in kindergarten there, Rikki decided to make a book. The work was completely her own. She was the one who came up with the initial idea and with the storyline. And she was responsible for the whole process – handwriting the words, illustrating each page, and putting all together as a bound book. After having worked on it for some time, she set it aside. I do not know if she grew tired of it and she just needed a break, if she wanted time to think about what to write next, if she was more interested in other work, or what. But it did not matter. Creating the book had been her own idea – not one imposed by her teachers; taking a break was also her idea – not one needing teacher's permission.

One teacher did not agree. She told Rikki that because it had lain idle for so long, if she did not work on it that day, it would be tossed. Rikki did not work on it that day, so into the garbage it went.

There are several issues here. First, why did it matter how long it had been left untouched? Do not adult writers leave works unfinished for periods of time? As long as there is no deadline – and there was none for Rikki, as the book was solely her responsibility – why should another care if it is worked on or left untouched for any length of time?

Second, why should the work be thrown out if it is not worked on? Was that the only option available? Certainly, there are other possibilities. If the teacher just could not stand to have an unfinished work in the classroom, the book could have been sent home.

Finally, why should the teacher throw out anything a student has done? This was an utterly disrespectful act. Even to threaten to do so if not worked on showed total lack of respect for Rikki and her work.

Rikki, with watery eyes, told me about this incident when I picked her up. My immediate conference with the teacher was revealing. Her ultimatum, she felt, had been right. It was within her bounds to determine whether a project had been left idle too long. And while she was sorry for having thrown out Rikki's work, it was only because she now realized how important it was to Rikki. That any child's work is important to its creator was not what she learned but only that this one piece was important to Rikki.

For me but not for Rikki, the teacher retrieved the booklet. As it had been thrown into the garbage, it was ruined. Any joy in continuing to write and illustrate the story was destroyed. What the teacher had said through her actions was that Rikki's work was garbage. What she said with words was that children's work was not worth saving.

I found the disrespect demonstrated by Rikki's teacher to be incredible. One would expect a teacher to have more understanding of her students than that. Working with children five days a week should certainly have let her realize that children value what they put time and energy into. Yet her attitude was no different from that of most adults. If it is child's work, it is worthless; only adult work has value.

Children *are* important. What they do is important. What they say is important. Because they are younger and less accomplished and less articulate than adults does not negate this. Nor are these statements true only in the child's eyes. Qualifiers are irrelevant. The child is important, period. To provide him with the dignity he needs, we recognize this point. Simply put, he is due our respect.

Chapter 7

Trust Gone Awry

I had a little pony,
His name was Grapple Gray.
I lent him to a lady
To ride him a mile away.
She whipped him, she lashed him,
She rode him through the mire.
I would not lend my pony now
For all the lady's hire.

There is, of course, the flip side to trusting one's child: the child may not live up to that trust.

Children are constantly checking the limits. What exactly are they, they wonder. Are they firm? What are the consequences of going beyond? Even when they know certain rules are solid, some children will still test the rules.

And in some ways this *is* what we want. While some parents want their children to grow into soldierly obedience, many want independence of thought. Independent thinking often leads to breaking the rules or, at the least, going against the tide. This applies not only to laws passed by legislative bodies. It relates also to what is done in one's profession. Casting the "You should do it this way" and "This is how we have always done it" aside leaves open the possibility for new insights, better methods, wondrous discoveries. This is no less true for children than for working adults. Children need opportunities to explore independence.

Adolescence, especially, is a time of herd mentality. Pressure is strong for all in the group (gang, clique, club, or whatever) to behave in a certain way. This may take an innocuous form, such as modes of dress. Oversized pants go against the commonly accepted Western dress code of clothes looking trim, neat, and well-fitting. Although the adult rules are being broken, the rules of the group are adhered to. And it is the peer group that has far more influence on the youth.

It is when the group norm takes on the more harmful or even dangerous forms that concern rises. Dress styles are one matter. Drug use, alcohol intake, premarital sex are something else altogether. One trained to follow the rules may choose the wrong ones. Rather than society's rules, it may more likely be the group's rules that are followed. The group bond is immediate and strong. Members are expected to act as a unit, gathering together, expressing similar thoughts, engaging in like activities. Deviations from their norm are a threat to this solidarity.

So when an otherwise good group of guys decides to experiment with drugs, what is your child to do? If independence of thought has been encouraged, he will openly examine this new stage. Rather than adhering to group rules, he will question this one's appropriateness.

But his response will depend on much more. How secure he is in himself will play a large part in deciding whether or not to stay with the group. Feeling uncomfortable because of independent thought does not guarantee that the questionable activity will be avoided. His need to remain part of the group may be stronger than his desire to do what he knows is proper. His position in the group will be important. Is he a leader whose opinion is respected? Or is he a follower? Whether he sees any options other than to go along with the group or else to drop out will matter. Maybe some ideas in middle ground will surface. Whether he *can* safely remove himself from this group or activity will be a consideration.

Being able to impartially assess the ramifications of proposed activities is, then, only part of what the child needs in order to act properly. But it is a first and crucial part. The above scenario fits adolescence. With drug experimentation, alcohol abuse, and sexual activity filtering into the middle school and even elementary years, parents of children of all ages need be concerned. There is no reason to focus on gangs. Sometimes all a child needs is another child to lead him the wrong way. Or sometimes it is not even being led but just willingness to go along with another that turns into trouble.

When my son, Ty, was ten, he had some unfortunate experiences. He and his friend took money from the friend's parents, went to the corner store, and loaded up on candy. This was not a one-time occurrence. It went on many times over several weeks. In fact, the boys bought so much candy that several years later the store owner was willing to give "good" customer Ty a discount on other, above-board purchases.

Several things were wrong here. Obviously, the boys had abused the trust we parents had put in them. They had stolen money. They had purchased candy – not allowed by either family. They had eaten sweets at a time, between meals, not ordinarily permitted. At least they had not eaten it all; the excess was stashed in secret spots outdoors.

Since Ty was the older boy by two years, he was, I felt, more at fault here. He should have been a leader in a positive way. Instead, he had readily joined in the deception. It was fun. Not only did he get whatever candy he wanted, but also he got it for free. And no one knew, at least not right away.

When we parents did discover what the boys had been up to, the consequences were immediate. They did not play with each other for many weeks. Money from their own savings went for repayment. The remaining hidden candy was retrieved and thrown out. And worst of all for Ty, because my trust in him had been shattered, he no longer enjoyed the freedom he had until then.

More than anything, that latter point was what I most wanted emphasized. Certainly, what he had done was wrong. We all make mistakes. Often, we can make up for them. But when we break the trust given us by others, that trust is not so quickly reestablished. To destroy that trust takes but a moment. To earn it back takes months. Every action on Ty's part now became questioned; assumptions that he would behave properly were no longer valid. Worse, since he could not be trusted on his own, he had to spend more time with me as I went about the more mundane chores of shopping, carpooling, or other away-from-home errands.

In some ways, the fact that what Ty did was relatively bad (worse, for example, than a single lie or taking a candy from a sibling), ensured that he would not give a repeat performance. Not surprisingly, Ty has repeatedly volunteered that he would never do anything like that again. In fact, once he had earned back our trust, he became a model boy.

Ty is, of course, not perfect. But the experience did provide positive benefits. He came to understand how important our trust in him is. He learned how quickly that trust can be wiped out. And he realized what is expected of him, especially in providing a positive role model for younger children.

Yet the education was not only on his part. It was an eye-opening experience for me, too. How the trust one gives to a child translates to everyday activity varies. Just as one would not allow a child to play unsupervised with a knife if the child has had no experience with using one, so, too, one does not give vast hours of unsupervised freedom to a child who is not used to it.

At the time of Ty's transgressions, I was spending many hours a day transporting his sisters to their classes. It often involved more than four hours a day away from home. Reluctant to confine Ty to the car for so long, I let him stay at home. That in itself could have been all right. But I ignored the clues Ty gave me that such an arrangement was not in his best interests.

In this case, Ty told me several times that he was bored. Such a statement is rare from my children. This was clearly Ty's cry for help and some adult direction. Other clues became obvious in retrospect. Lack of an appetite at dinner was common, thanks to the candy eaten in the afternoon, but it was uncharacteristic and should have been questioned. Ty's spending much time in a certain location where the candy was hidden should also have been investigated as it was not a normal play area for either boy.

Had I been more aware and, especially, present, these clues would have registered, and appropriate action would have occurred much earlier. As it was, while Ty was "doing time" for his offenses, I, too, changed my behavior. I became more actively involved and more aware of Ty's activities – where he was, what he was doing, whom he was with. With some children such action might seem overbearing and intrusive. But each child is different, and each child has periods of differing needs. At this point in his life, Ty still needed a parent nearby for much of the day. It was not necessarily to have an adult actively involved with him all day long. But his need was at least to have an adult available. Sometimes when one is young, it helps to have an obvious, physical manifestation of one's conscience. A parent who sets the rules and limits readily fulfills that role.

In the previous example, Ty not only needed adult help but also realized he had such a need and called out for it. His statements about being bored were his way of seeking assistance. Given that such pronouncements were otherwise rare for him, they indicated deeper problems that he was having.

This is the key to discovering that problems exist. When behavior is out of the ordinary for that child, it is often because a deeper, seemingly unrelated problem exists. This was so, also, when Ty went through his bedwetting stage. For him, bedwetting was an anomaly. It was not a problem he had had all along but, instead, started happening after more than a year of dry nights. So the behavior stood out there just as did his comments here about boredom. It is not bedwetting or being bored, per se, that indicates something is wrong. It is, instead, the context of the behavior, its relativity. Is it unusual? Does it stand out? And playing upon a parent's intuition, does it just not seem right?

Children are rarely totally deceptive in such matters. They want to be found out; they know something is not right; they truly want help. It is just that they cannot say so directly. It, then, is the parent's job to recognize these hidden cries. This can be done only by knowing one's child. And this is best accomplished by being around him. By being familiar with what is normal for one's own child, one can see what is not normal; it will stand out.

Chapter 8

On Their Own

I can tie my shoelace.
I can comb my hair.
I can wash my hands and face
And dry myself with care.

I can brush my teeth, too,
And button up my frocks.
I can say, "How do you do?"
And put on both my socks.

As much as children need and want our help, they also need to solve problems on their own. Often they know which situations they can handle themselves even if their well-intentioned parents do not.

I am the oldest of five children. Next in line is one of my brothers. Growing up, he and I frequently fought, not only verbally argued but also physically fought hand and fist. One day at about age 12, I realized the folly of it all. We would hit and hurt, but nothing was ever changed. The fighting, I realized, did not solve a thing. The bad feelings were just carried over to later when we would start all over again.

Unfortunately, my timing for acting upon this insight was not the greatest. This realization came to me in the midst of a fight. As we exchanged blows, I understood how stupid it was to fight because it never solved anything for us. So I stopped. My hands were stilled. But my brother's were not. He had had no such insight, so he continued to hammer away at me. I was quite incensed that he had not caught on, that he had not realized why I had stopped, and that he had taken advantage of me.

Although that fight did not end well for me, it was essentially our last fight. My refraining from fighting had nothing to do with punishments from our parents for our fighting. It was not related to refereeing on their parts. Nor was it due to lectures about solving our sibling disputes some other way. I just finally understood the senselessness of it. I had had sufficient experience with fighting my brother and with seeing what resulted from these fights. With this understanding came positive action. I believe this insight is called growing up.

My own children rarely had physical fights. Instead, they bickered, which annoyed me as much, I suspect, as my youthful fights had irritated by parents. And like them, I felt obligated to interfere and lend them my negotiating assistance. Having weathered growing up with four siblings, I felt sufficiently experienced in handling childhood disagreements.

Sadly, my good intentions were not well received.

At one point, Rikki and Rhiannon, about six and eight years old, respectively, had been arguing for sometime. Weary of hearing their verbal attacks, I interrupted them, ready to solve their latest irresolvable issue. It was not to be. Quite rightly, Rhiannon responded with, "Mom, leave us alone. We can take care of this ourselves."

Admittedly, I was offended that my services were not wanted. But I soon realized the wisdom of Rhiannon's statement.

What do children learn when the parent interferes in their disagreements? Some would maintain that children learn how to negotiate, how to settle differences, and how to solve problems wisely and verbally. By watching and listening to the parent, they say, children learn negotiating skills.

It just is not so. Instead, children learn to seek outside help when their differences seem unsolvable. In the adult's world, such help comes with attorney fees attached. In the children's world, they learn that they are not capable so must seek someone else with appropriate expertise or power.

Left alone to settle their dispute themselves, children are forced to come up with a solution. They must often be creative in devising a solution that neither one had originally proposed. This is called "compromise," where each gives a little and neither one wins all. "Okay, we'll play your game for half an hour, then the one I want for the next half hour." Or, "We'll start over and agree on the rules before we begin again."

Sometimes, the solution is not a compromise but a termination. "I don't want to play any more." The problem involves a lack of trust or a violation of it: "He cheated" versus "I did not." No arbitrator can determine who is speaking the truth. It may very well be that the best solution is as the children have declared. Not to play together for a while gives each the chance to cool off, forget differences, and then feel the need to get back together. There is no reason two playing together must do so until a set time. Nor is there a rule that a game once begun must be finished. Pauses in play, however long, are perfectly permissible.

Such a solution may run counter to what the parent believes is best. The tendency is to declare a ruling based on how the adult interprets the situation. For instance, the younger child of the two may not necessarily be the innocent one although parents tend to give the younger one the benefit of the doubt. Regardless, by siding with one, the parent is sure to draw the resentment of the other child. Play may be forced to continue since the parent has ruled. But all is not well. With one party feeling ignored or not believed, resentment will linger and retaliation is sure to follow. The supposed solution then becomes only temporary as another altercation follows.

Even if the interfering parent does not take sides but, instead, reaches what she feels is a compromise, bad feelings can persist. It is due to the fact that an outsider has imposed the ruling, and the outsider rarely understands all of the nuances of what led to the disagreement in the first place. It may be a solution that pleases neither child. ("No, we do not want to start the game over; it will take too long.") Or it may be one that seems even-handed to the adult, but which actually sides with one of the children. ("No, I don't want to start the game over. I was winning, but since we didn't finish, the game won't really count. If we start over, I might not win.")

Nor does it work to ask the children if the adult's solution is agreeable to both sides. The children know the adult wants her authority recognized. The correct response, they know, is to submit to the ruling. After all, their disagreement has already resulted in her displeasure and subsequent interference. To disagree with her now would not improve the situation. So the children unwillingly submit. But here, too, resentment remains, and more disagreements will likely arise.

This is no different than what happens in the adult work place. Decisions that are reached based upon the input of all workers are much more readily accepted and implemented. In contrast, rulings imposed from above are often met with derision and, worse, noncompliance. It is a question of power and control. When decisions come from above – the boss, teacher, parent – one feels powerless.

For the child, the fact that some of the house rules are set by the parent is fine. The child does not want to be involved in every decision to be made any more than does the employee. So many just are not important enough. But when the matter bears directly upon him, he will want a say. Certainly, this is so when the ruling has the potential to call into question his honesty or ability or intelligence or some other aspect of how he defines himself.

Many of these arguments are, after all, minor. Why bother getting involved? If the bickering becomes annoying to the adult ears, the adult can move away or have the children take their quarrel elsewhere.

The purpose of such arguing is not simply to reach an agreement. It is also to learn how to reach that agreement. Listening to a third party does not serve this purpose. It is a situation similar to one where an impatient speaker does not listen to the one preceding him. Instead, he thinks only about what he will say and waits for the first sign of a break where he can interject his opinion.

So here, too, with a refereeing adult, the bickering two wait impatiently for the referee to stop talking. Each cares only to get his point across, which invariably is justification for him being right (or less wrong) and the other being at fault. There is no attempt to understand the other viewpoint; there is no listening to the other explanation, except to wait for a pause to continue his own discourse. Any appeals are naturally made to this third party rather than to the one with whom he is at odds.

Consider the alternative. With no referee, appeals for justice, fairness, and understanding must be made directly to the opposition. And the opposition already knows most of the facts – who did what and did it when. What is lacking is a comprehension of why – the reason for the action, the feeling behind the words, the assumptions mistakenly made.

Not all one-on-one disagreements will be resolved. Not all will be resolved fairly. As one learns, mastery is not immediately assured. It takes time to figure out what works. And it often takes a few failures to understand that successes are more desirable. If failure to resolve the issue means the friend goes away, there will be incentive to reach an agreement next time so that play can continue. If each does not want to give in, it will take awhile for one or both even to want to consider compromise. In the end, it becomes a question of how much one gives up – of one's ego, of one's winning position, of one's commitment to a specific course of action – versus how much one wants to play with the other.

An adult cannot weigh those two sides for either child. Each must come to his own conclusion. What the adult *can* do is be available when both children are at a standstill. That is, when both have tried to resolve their problem but cannot find a solution, they can appeal to a third party. This works only if both want assistance. Otherwise, with only one wanting adult interference, the other will not accept the adult's suggestion or ruling.

Sometimes, the adult can offer insight the children usually overlook. But this is offered, not imposed. It is up to the children to accept it.

My son, Ty, and a friend would frequently play games at our house on weekends. Just as frequently, the friend would leave because of some disagreement. On his way out of our house one time, I asked why he was leaving. Once again, it was because of a dispute over a game. "Why not," I proposed to him, "work out the problem instead of leaving?"

Much to my surprise, the boy paused, considered, and then decided to stay. It was as if he had never thought about even trying to resolve a disagreement. Instead, he had just left. His way of dealing with disputes was to walk out on them.

He is not the only child I have found to avoid resolving an issue. Sometimes, it is easier to leave and not participate in what may very well be a lengthy discussion. And if compromise is seen as the most likely solution, by leaving, the child maintains his point; he does not give in, does not lose face. What he is saying, ultimately, is that rather than work out the problem with the other child, he would prefer to play alone.

There is, of course, nothing wrong with playing by oneself. What is wrong is to develop the habit of always avoiding solving problems. In this boy's case, it seemed to be a habit to the extent that alternatives were not even considered. Maybe that is why my suggestion was taken. It was novel, a possibility to be entertained, at least, if not actually tried.

As much as I felt always running away from disagreements was not in either child's best interests, I was prepared to accept a rejection of my suggestion. It is hardly a suggestion if the child must carry it out. To enforce compliance would just set us back to the point previously discussed where adults constantly referee.

It must also be mentioned that some children enjoy arguing. Ty and one friend in particular seem to be always engaged in a battle of words. Despite my years of hearing the bickering of the children, I am not completely comfortable listening to such go on and on. In exasperation, I once asked the boys if they actually enjoy arguing as they do it so much. Much to my surprise, they readily admitted that they do. And on several subsequent occasions, Ty has volunteered that he especially enjoys arguing with this friend. For these two, it is more like sparring with words. They are exercising their verbal expertise; they are practicing convincing another with just words; they are trying out different techniques that may carry over to other areas of their lives.

There is much to be said for allowing this to continue. Certainly, matching wits has merit over matching fists. It is a safe way to deal with differences. Both boys are good friends, and these verbal disputes are always friendly. The only real problem was with my intolerance for hearing them in their debates. As I now know to tune them out, that is a problem no more.

Apart from the annoyance of hearing children arguing, many parents are uncomfortable in letting children resolve disputes by themselves. They fear that one of them may be taken advantage of. Adults are needed, they believe, to ensure fairness of decisions.

Consider the alternative where adults are not involved. Ty would often play Monopoly® with one of his friends. Since at this time Ty could not read but his friend could, the friend did all of the reading in the game. Later when he had learned how to read, Ty realized that his friend had been most creative in his reading. No wonder Ty had always lost. His friend had always read the cards in his favor and against Ty's, regardless of what was actually printed on the cards.

So what was the result of adults staying out of this game? Obviously, Ty always lost. But he still enjoyed playing the game. Clearly, winning was not the only reason for his playing. His friend, too, enjoyed the game. But for him, the winning may well have been the point in playing. Would an interfering adult have allowed him to enjoy playing as much and without regard for the outcome of the game? I doubt it.

Even though Ty was the one taken advantage of, he came out ahead, I believe. He learned to enjoy the game for its own sake, win or lose. And he learned something about his friend that a refereeing adult would not have taught him. He learned that the boy cheats, that he engages in dishonest activity to win, that he is not to be trusted or, at least, is to be watched suspiciously. Had an adult intervened, the extent of the boy's dishonesty would not have been evident. It would have been seen as a one-time occurrence. As it was, Ty was (eventually) put on guard and realized his friend could cheat in any game. Despite the cheating, having an adult ensure fairness would have meant a less enjoyable game. Every card drawn by Ty or his friend would have to have been read by the adult. So an adult would have had to be nearby *and* willing to be constantly interrupted.

Would Ty's friend have been better off with an adult overseeing the game? While he would have been prevented from cheating in this game, he would likely not have stopped cheating elsewhere. (Indeed, this was supported in other situations that later came to light.) Would an interfering adult have let the boy learn to enjoy playing the game as much as winning at it?

In this case, it seems unlikely. At home, the boy has been taught the importance of winning. That is what is enjoyable about playing; that is *the* reason to play. A differing viewpoint, such as the pleasure of just playing with a friend, would not take precedent over what had been learned from his parents. So an outsider would have little influence over the boy's internalized reasons for playing the game. And it is certainly unlikely that his parents would change their thinking on this subject. At best, an outsider would merely be a referee, influencing only the externalities. Only while his behavior was monitored would there be a change. But because it would come from outside of him, the change would be temporary. Remove the external, monitoring adult, and he would revert back to his normal win-at-any-costs behavior.

But, even then, what an intervening adult would have done is place the emphasis on winning. After all, that is why fair play is a major consideration. It ensures that each has an equal opportunity to win. Further, the adult would have made the game onerous, as play would be constantly interrupted for the adult to read everything that came up in the course of the game. Even more, an adult would likely have to watch the game to make sure cheating did not occur otherwise.

This is not to say that children should cheat or even that players should not worry if opponents cheat. It is to say that in such games children will learn, all on their own, how to deal with less than proper behavior. They will learn that some people will cheat, so one must be alert and wary. They will learn about the character of specific individuals. They will learn play can be fun even if opponents are not fair players. This latter point is certainly an important one for anyone who plays sports to learn. Invariably, referees make bad calls. To be so wrapped up in calling each play correctly will inevitably detract from enjoyment in the game.

Consider another instance involving supposed foul play.

Card games were all the rage. As enthusiastic supporters of all things Star Wars™, Ty and his friends were no less taken with the Star Wars™ card game. Cards were bought, sold, and traded. One friend, Dan, collected the cards based upon their pictures. More sophisticated players collected cards based upon how valuable the card was or whether it would make their playing deck more powerful. Dan and another of

Ty's friends made a trade with each other. Dan got a card that had a picture he liked; the other boy got a card he needed to make his deck better in games with others. Each got what he wanted.

In this case, an adult intervened. Feeling Dan had been cheated, his parents made both boys exchange back their cards. Each card has a value, published in a periodical, and Dan's card given to the other boy was more valuable than the one he got.

Were the boys helped by this intervention? It seems not at all. In the original trade, Dan had gotten a card he wanted. That its published value was less than the one he gave in exchange was irrelevant. He had a value system different from the card manufacturer's. The other boy's value system was in line with the card manufacturer's, so he felt he was getting a good deal also. By undoing the trade, the parents undid what both boys had considered a good and fair trade.

Further, because Dan's parents were afraid that their son would be taken advantage of again (even though the boy felt it had not happened even once), they forbade him from doing any other trades without their approval. This is just the situation that was avoided in the Monopoly® game by parents not getting involved. So here, every time Dan wanted to trade, he had to run to his parents, have them check both cards on the list to ensure an equal trade, then return to his friends with an approval or rejection. This was not fun for anyone – parents, Dan, or friends. And, as the infamous trade showed, this interference assured all parties of a fair trade only in terms of the manufacturer's list. Having differing criteria, as Dan did, meant that what were fair trades according to the adults were not necessarily so to Dan.

In the end, all Dan learned was to run to his parents. Even then, it assured him of a trade that was fair only according to others. Ignored was his idea of a fair trade.

Had his parents listened to Dan, they would have learned that he had his own, equally valid system for evaluating the cards for trade. As long as the cards were his (they were) and bought with his own money or given as gifts (this was also true), why not let him handle them as he desired? In fact, would he not learn more by setting up trades by his own criteria rather than relying on a published list? He would certainly have to be creative, inventive, and independent in setting up values himself for each card.

Obviously, the parents had their son's best interests in mind. Since he was younger and less accomplished, he was vulnerable to being taken advantage of. But by making him dependent upon their approval for any trades, they assured him of further dependency as well as continued vulnerability. Had he been allowed to trade unencumbered by parents, he would have learned how to trade on his own. He would have learned, as did the other boys, from his mistakes.

This is key to what parents most fear: that the child will make a mistake and get hurt (or worse) or be cheated. There are, of course, some fears that are well founded. A toddler rarely understands that streets are dangerous and play should be restricted only to one side with no unassisted crossing of the road. Most parents understand this. That is, they understand their toddler is incapable of assessing the dangers of the street, of checking for traffic on the street, of capably determining the speed of the oncoming vehicles versus his own speed in crossing. They also know that the danger is extreme; the child could be killed from a miscalculation made in crossing.

Problems arise when the danger is less extreme and the parents' understanding of the child is wanting. In the case with Dan, the danger was minimal. It was certainly not life-threatening or even physically threatening. Nor was it a danger to his self-esteem. If anything, having to use his parents for his trades became an affront to his self-confidence. He now had to rely upon them. Before, he was one of the boys, on a par with them in that he could make trades on his own. Likely, the only danger to Dan in this case was that a bad trade would mean a loss of a card worth at most $25 but purchased for far less. But that would be so only according to his parents. By using his own valuation for the cards and doing the trades himself, Dan would not make a bad trade. Of course, in Dan's eyes, the only danger was in his parents' interfering. And that was due to his parents not understanding him.

Had they truly understood, they would have realized that it is by doing that learning best takes place. Watching or listening to another just does not measure up. To merely watch or listen to another allows the bystander to tune out. I have certainly seen often enough that glazed look when children have been subjected to informational lectures. Any interest in the topic quickly dissipates. But even if the child is interested and does listen, the degree of understanding will be less if active involvement is not allowed.

When the child is actively engaged, he is using all of his resources. He is the one thinking, analyzing, doing. He is the one figuring out what works and what does not. He may have heard lectures aplenty, but no amount of parental wisdom can possibly cover all likely circumstances. Invariably, there will be instances where he must judge for himself and react appropriately. In this way, he is part of the whole process. It is not just a matter of doing what someone else has told him to do. Instead, he understands that, based on the incident, ideas are generated, rejected, reconsidered, reformulated. Action is taken. Its impact is, in turn, analyzed, and further action is taken. By doing all, the child better understands the *why* of the process. But when merely told what to do, this understanding eludes the child. And without understanding, he cannot apply this experience to future circumstances. It is a dead-end with no growth or learning for the child, only continual dependence upon a parent.

That a child learns by doing is obvious for physical accomplishments. For instance, in riding a bike, we can describe all the points to remember, but it is only when the child climbs aboard and tries on his own that any progress is made. Even then, it seems more a matter of just *doing* rather than consciously *thinking* of all that is involved. To be aware of it all is too much – pedal, hold on, keep balanced, banish thoughts of falling, keep going, look ahead, etc.

That a child learns equally well when it is not a physical endeavor is not as readily accepted. Yet learn the child does. It may not happen as quickly as, say, learning to ride a bike. And the fact that learning is occurring may not be as evident as in mastering a physical task. Yet when the encounter is a verbal exchange or on an emotional level, practice of skills in these areas just as readily leads to mastery by the child.

Ty demonstrated this especially well to us several years ago. Like most children, he has had vast experience solving his own problems. Even though we parents like to get involved, there are many instances where we just are not aware of the problems a child may be having. It may be minor, and there is no point in telling us. It may happen when we are away. It may be too embarrassing to talk about. Or it may even be that the child cannot articulate what went on.

In this case, we had just acquired a seven-week-old puppy. Ty was four at the time. We had seen the puppy's sister at a beach park and played with it before deciding to get its sibling. Much to his fear, Ty found our puppy to be just like its sister in one unfortunate regard. It loved to nibble on bare, little toes. Being a puppy, Bo had sharp puppy teeth that hurt when biting Ty's bare skin. Covering up with socks or even shoes did not help as the teeth could penetrate the material. Worse, he loved to lick faces. Ty's sisters enjoyed that; Ty did not. Being not much farther off the ground than the puppy, Ty found it frightening to have a dog come toward his face with its mouth open. Still worse, since among family members Ty's face was closest to the dog's level, Ty was approached more often than anyone else.

As we worked on proper behavior for the puppy (such as getting him to nibble only on designated, inanimate items), Ty worked on his own behavior. For the first week, he sought shelter on the couch whenever Bo romped in the house. He was clearly frightened of the dog.

But Ty knew both he and the dog would be living in the same house, and he did not want to be confined to the couch for the next many years.

This is how Ty overcame his fears. First, he joined the rest of us in teaching Bo not to jump up on him or other people. He would tell him "No!" whenever he did something wrong. This gave Ty the feeling that he was in charge – or at least eventually would be – in regard to the dog. The dog should obey him, and he was practicing teaching him that he was a top dog, at least relative to Bo.

He also petted Bo. He began by doing it when Bo was asleep and within reach of his sanctuary, the couch. He progressed to standing on the floor and petting while Bo was otherwise engaged, as in play with the girls. He also worked on the mental aspects of his fear. He would say "Bo is a nice dog" or "I like Bo." The fear was still there, but Ty realized he had to accept him, embrace him, even, in order to get over his fear.

All of this four-year-old Ty did on his own. We did not suggest what to do or say. Nor did we push him to pet the dog or play with him. Nor would embarrassing him have helped. Pointing out his fear, telling him it is silly to be afraid of a little puppy, reminding him he is bigger would have been only counterproductive. As it was, Ty knew how best to deal with his fear. He pushed himself; there was no need for us to do so. Working from his comfort zone, he gradually stretched that boundary by doing slightly more each day. And he knew to work not only on physically dealing with the dog but also with his mental acceptance of him.

Having mastered this fear himself, Ty was far better off than had we intervened. No one knew where Ty's comfort zone was except him. Had we parents tried to stretch it, we likely would have guessed wrong and either pushed him to do too much with Bo or not challenged him enough, and, thus, Ty would have made no progress. Had we been by his side working together on his fear, we would have made him dependent upon us for this. Where would be the point when he can do it himself? By knowing that he can handle the situation without us, he is in a better position when he must deal with fears and we are not around.

Finally, by not getting involved, we did not make this fear overly important. It is like running and falling and scraping a knee. It is no big deal; one just gets up and carries on. Here, the fear is no big deal; one handles it and carries on. To otherwise dwell on it, discuss it, and work on it with Mommy makes it more important and, in the child's eye, overwhelming. It then becomes even more difficult to master. As it was, to Ty, it was just one other problem to work on when he felt ready.

Sometimes the problems are not so readily handled on a physical level. Nor are they as identifiable as a problem to the child. These are ones he is less likely to be able to articulate. Since the child cannot talk about what is troubling him, the parent is in a difficult position to help. But because he cannot describe what is bothering him, the child is not at a loss for helping himself. Subconsciously, he often knows what is needed.

As was mentioned previously, Ty went through a period where he needed more time with his father than he was getting. This resulted in, among other things, bedwetting. While I was initially at a loss to determine what was really bothering Ty, he took solace in certain stories. There was one bedtime story that must have especially struck the right chord, for he asked for it again and again and again. It was *Jack and the Beanstalk*.

As everyone knows, *Jack and the Beanstalk* is about a boy who sells the family cow for magic beans that grow into a sky-high beanstalk. Jack climbs the beanstalk to a giant's world, takes advantage of a giantess' kindness, and steals from her husband. In the end, the boy is rich and has killed the giant.

It has become popular of late to revise such classic tales. In these retellings, gender of key players is changed; stories do not always end happily ever after; heroes and villains become more complex and less one-sided. By so tampering with stories that have stood the test of time, revisionists risk destroying the meaning that listeners can otherwise derive from the tales.

For this fairy tale, I have known parents to change the story line so that either Jack is punished for stealing or else he acquires the goods honestly. Others change the boy into a girl. Such changes miss the point of the story or, I should say, the many points of the story.

Each child gets from this or any other fairy tale that which is important to him at that point in time. When Ty felt he needed more time with his father, he also felt anger at him for not giving him what was so important to him. He felt frustrated, powerless, unable to change the situation. This is a feeling young children often have. They are all too aware of just how little and powerless they are in an adult world.

The story *Jack and the Beanstalk* spoke to Ty (and speaks to any child) in a way no parent could. It worked on a subconscious level to ease what was bothering him. Here in the fairy tale is a little boy taking on the giant – and winning. It is what Ty wanted. To him it was not a story about stealing; it was not teaching him dishonest ways; it was not telling him to take advantage of others. It was simply easing his pain in being little and powerless. It gave him hope that his littleness and powerlessness would not last forever. And so he asked to hear it over and over again.

Another source of solace to Ty was the story "The Son of the Ogress" (from *Folk Tales and Fables of Asia & Australia*). This less familiar tale from India also hit several right spots for Ty. In this story, a giantess-monster captures a man, but rather than eat him, marries him and has a child by him. She keeps both her husband and son in her cave while she goes out by day. She loves them both and tries to adapt to their ways. But it is no use. They are unhappy, and she knows that in order to keep them she must use force. Eventually, through the boy's initiative and the strength inherited from his mother, the father and son escape. The story ends with the boy, with the aid of a talisman given him by his mother, meeting with extraordinary success. Given that during this time Ty had more than enough time with Mom and most wanted to be just with his dad, the relevance of this fairy tale is obvious.

My point here is not to show how fairy tales help a child cope with life's problems. The danger would be in overanalyzing every story a child wants to hear. We can never know fully what is going on in another's mind, even in our own child's mind. And when the appeal is to the subconscious, we are on even shakier ground in such analysis. In a way, too, such analysis can be overly intrusive. We all need some privacy. Except in extreme cases, our children deserve no less.

What I do wish to illustrate with these examples is that such stories often have meaning well beyond the superficial story line. Children will derive benefit from them in ways we cannot always know or anticipate. And we do not have to know what the deeper meaning is for them. It is enough that it happens.

Nor should we believe that because a child is of a certain age or past a specific stage in life that a favored story is no longer needed. It is the child's needs that must be honored. We cannot be sure that the child is truly past a certain stage in growing up. Maybe he no longer fears the dark, but monsters in the night are not totally subdued in his mind. He may still be working on problems that to us appear already solved. There is great pressure in our society to appear brave, strong, and in control. The outward appearance given may well fit such expectations. What is really felt may be another matter entirely. Such fairy tales may be one means the child uses to make reality fit expectation.

We cannot be sure in what ways a fairy tale affects the child – beyond the obvious liking or not liking it. We do not know what aspects of it appeal to him. Nor can we know if the appeal will be consistent over time. To fiddle with the story, then, is to risk destroying what the child needs most from it. These are tales that have come down to us from generations past. They have been told over and over again and have remained favorites with children worldwide. And this has been so without glorious illustrations. It is the words that speak to the child; pictures are superfluous. With words alone, the child's mind is free to imagine – to see himself as the girl in the story or herself as the boy, to see the giant as his dad, to see his mom as the monster. In this way, the story becomes his own more so than when there are pictures that show exactly what the main characters look like.

There is also the risk that in altering the story we will emphasize what is not important. For instance, in some stories, the main character is a boy. Changing it to a girl says that the gender matters in the story. Often it does not. The main character, girl or boy, merely represents a child. And the listener, whether girl or boy, will respond to the story in that way. That is, the significance of the story will be felt independent of the character's gender (or race or age or socioeconomic background). Changing the character to a specific gender signals to the listener that the story really is about, for instance, just girls in such situations. The story loses its universality. Making such changes also puts emphasis on the externalities of the story. Invariably, the attraction is to the underlying themes.

This is all to say that when a child requests the same story for the gazillionth time, we need to retrieve our last iota of patience and read it to him. Sometimes, it is just a good story that he likes so much he is working on memorizing it. Other times, it is a story that speaks to him in a way no adult conversation ever can. We cannot be sure which it is. And it should not matter. In either case, it is a need. It is our job to fill it.

Because we do not know which stories a child most needs at any given point, we do well to expose him to many fairy tales and myths. That way, he has a full repertoire upon which to draw. As he works to solve one more weighty problem, he can request that story which addresses his need. This allows him to solve the problem himself, albeit with the parent reading the words. But it is his identification of the story he needs that is important. Hearing the words helps. But he can, thanks to the repeated readings, replay the story in his mind as he needs it.

Stories can help. But they are not the only solution. Children have incredible resources within themselves that can help them in various circumstances. This was demonstrated by my children in a situation common to many American youngsters.

Each of my children, when young, sucked fingers rather than a pacifier. (Yes, each one sucked on two fingers, not a thumb, and each chose ones different from his or her siblings.) Parents who give their child a pacifier often control its use and eventually its discontinuation. This is not so readily done when fingers are used instead. And that is how I preferred it. I reasoned that when the need for the comfort and security derived from sucking on the fingers was no longer there, the child would end the practice. I realized that the sucking could become a habit which would be harder to stop. But I still felt the child could control it.

The risk here was that the child would continue sucking well past the age at which it is commonly accepted. Or worse, it might never stop.

All three children stopped on their own. And all three stopped when they were seven years old. Rikki was almost seven and a half when she decided to quit sucking her fingers. They still tasted good to her (as she explained to me). She did not want to lose that good taste completely, so she decided to phase out her sucking. First, she stopped sucking during the day. This allowed her the comfort of sucking at night when no one else was around.

Unfortunately, while engaging in this only at nighttime, Rikki was keeping the taste "alive." Her older sister confirmed this. Rhiannon mentioned how, as long as she had kept sucking her fingers, however infrequently, she remained used to it and wanted to continue. So Rikki was making a complete cessation harder to accomplish by doing it in stages.

I could have intervened, or at least tried to do so, by somehow preventing her evening sucking. But where would have been the benefit? It would have been a terrible struggle for the two of us. And it would have been just at the time – bedtime – when a child most needs comfort, quiet, and happy, loving thoughts. It is not the time for confrontations.

More important, why should I have taken on what was, after all, her problem? If I were embarrassed by her sucking, *my* embarrassment would be *my* problem. Her sucking in no way harmed her. (Despite warnings, thumb-sucking does not contribute to crooked teeth. My oldest's naturally perfect teeth are a testament to that.) That some adults would be disturbed by it was not reason for me to have stopped her. Here, too, that would be their problem, not the child's.

If the child is embarrassed by finger- or thumb-sucking, that is the child's problem. If the child feels she is too old to be sucking, stopping is her problem. And it is one readily handled by the child.

Eventually, Rikki did stop sucking at night, too. She enjoyed a brief period of nighttime finger-sucking then realized what her older sister had found out: she had to stop completely. Once she did, the attraction to sucking fingers was gone forever. I asked her. She told me that the fingers just did not taste good any more. There was no turning back.

It was a relatively minor problem. It involved only Rikki. And she was fully capable of handling it. By dealing with such problems on their own, children acquire self-confidence. They realize how much they are capable of doing all by themselves. They learn creativity in coming up with appropriate solutions. And from mastery of simpler, more minor problems comes the ability and willingness to handle greater problems.

Children want self-mastery. They aspire to be adult-like, taking on problems and solving them. They know only too well how they compare to adults and how far they fall short of adult achievements. By taking on problems and solving them themselves, they move that much closer to adulthood. From the child's perspective, it is a long process. But every problem that the child solves on his own takes him that much closer to his goal.

How the child views this process and his place in it varies tremendously. As one example, John Holt mentioned how his young nephew (and any other child, he felt) viewed himself as incompetent compared to adults. The boy was well aware of how far he still had to travel to become as competent and capable as the grown-ups in his world. This was demonstrated when the boy's mother asked him how it felt to be four. "Perfectly ghastly" came the reply.

Not content with that evaluation as true for all children despite my great respect for the observations of Holt, I quizzed my own son. How did he feel about being four years old? His reply was a barely contained grin. He felt perfectly wonderful. It was several months after his fourth birthday, but he still felt the joy of being four and no longer only three.

I suspect more was at play there. Although still much a young child, Ty was constantly doing adult-like activities and doing them well: slicing bread, grating hard Parmesan cheese, sweeping the floor. Not everything he attempted he was able to do to his satisfaction. But there were enough successes for him to feel accomplished and competent. For him it was not a long, arduous road from incompetent childhood to capable adulthood. Instead, it was a wonderful journey full of successes.

Problems for a child are not just those we readily identify as such. They can be as minor as sweeping the floor. For months when I would pick Rikki up from her preschool-kindergarten, I would find her sweeping. She was truly a master sweeper by the time she graduated. And, yes, she used that skill often at home.

She also used that skill to earn money. When Rikki was young, she was doing yard work for a neighbor. Among several tasks, the job involved sweeping the sidewalk. Having swept, she was about to put the pile of sweeping in the trash. It was not to be so simple. The elderly neighbor had her own ideas of how it should be done. Her methods were probably fine, but so were Rikki's. After all, why should she care how it was done as long as it got done? It is not as if any damage or harm would come of alternative methods. Rikki proceeded to clean up in her own and equally effective way. But she felt quite insulted in being told how to do something so simple.

After performing a task innumerable times, we adults hardly think about what we are doing or why we are doing it in just such a way. Sometimes, our method is not even our own but has been handed down from one generation to the next. This can result in some odd habits. One friend always opened the oven door midway through baking anything because her grandmother always had done so. It was completely unnecessary and only caused the oven to lose heat. We get in a rut and fail to see other ways of operating and then fail to see better ways. This can happen to children, too, who stick with one method even though we believe better ones are available. So we can guide the child, showing him how to do it or how others do it. But we can also let him try on his own. And we can certainly let him adapt the procedure to what works best for him.

At home, there are many opportunities for a young child to do just that. Work that is familiar or even a tedious bore to us presents challenges for children who are just learning. We can present the problem, but it is up to the child to accept it. The child, too, decides how to tackle it and whether he wants adult assistance. "Do you want to grate the cheese?" It is up to the child. Does he want to be shown how? It is up to the child. After all, our way may not be the best, especially for a child with little hands. Success at such small tasks paves the way for success with greater problems.

It is a difficult role we parents take. On the one hand, we are wholly responsible for our children – for their safety, for their education, for their food and shelter. On the other hand, the children are the ones responsible for what they do, how they behave, the choices they make. We do not wish for them to tumble and fall, yet what child has learned to walk without hitting the ground many times? It is not so much that we protect them from falling. Failure, even if it hurts, is a part of life. It is that we guard against them falling too far. So a one-year-old learns to walk first on level ground where obstacles are out of the way. Only years later does that child attempt to walk a log spanning a rushing river.

We want the child to learn, so we provide what we believe is the proper environment. We set the outer boundaries – how far the child can wander from the house, how late he can stay up, what tools he can use, etc. We set them to allow as much freedom and exploration and growth as possible. Within those limits, the child is on his own. He decides how far from the house he will go without passing the set boundary. He decides what he will do with his time until bedtime. He decides how, when, and where he will use the tools. In this way, the child practices what he feels he needs to learn. He pushes himself to an extent compatible with his comfort level. It can be just beyond where he is comfortable when he feels ready to push. Or it can be still at that comfort zone when he is not quite ready to extend his limits. It is not always pushing at the boundaries, trying to expand them. It is more often working happily within those bounds, even at times resting. He is, after all, on his own.

Chapter 9

What's a Parent to Do?

Over in the meadow in the sand in the sun
Lived an old mother turtle and her little turtle one.
"Dig," said the mother. "We dig," said the one.
So they dug all day in the sand in the sun.

Over in the meadow where the stream runs blue
Lived an old mother fish and her little fishes two.
"Swim," said the mother. "We swim," said the two.
So they swam all day where the stream runs blue.

Over in the meadow in a hole in a tree
Lived an old mother owl and her little owlets three.
"Tu-whoo," said the mother. "Tu-whoo," said the three.
So they tu-whooed all day in a hole in a tree.

Life with our child is more a partnership than a dictatorship. Trying to exert total control over the child will work, if at all, for only a limited time. Look at bulimic girls who, in academics and extracurricular activities, are otherwise succeeding to please their parents. Control over their own lives is limited. So they exert control in one of the few ways they can – by surreptitiously expelling the food they have eaten.

To work for total control of the child is to deny that child's drive for independence, self-mastery, and self-realization.

Here is a small example. When Rikki was four years old, she was working on a puzzle. I saw that progress was slow so offered my help. I am a very orderly person, and that carries over into how I do puzzles. I first get the four corners, then all side pieces. Once the border is complete, I work toward the center using the colors of the pieces as my guide. I relayed this supreme wisdom to Rikki so she could better work her puzzle. Or, rather, I tried to help. She would have none of it. She had her own method, very different from mine. She fit pieces together based on their shapes. It seemed very tedious to me, but it was based on how she saw the pieces. Where I saw color as the dominant feature, Rikki saw shape.

So what was my role there? It was, or should have been, simply observer. No help was needed; none was requested; none should have been given. That is respect for the child. It seems that all invariably turns back to that — respect the child; trust the child. If there is a problem, the child will let us know in some way. Meanwhile, mastery is at work. And that is best accomplished when the child has control.

Total control? No. For instance, such a puzzle with small pieces would never be given to a toddler. The pieces would end up in his mouth. The puzzle would be ruined and, worse, the child could choke. In this partnership, the parent provides the proper environment. So it is a puzzle at or just above the child's ability. And it is access to the parent or another adult should assistance be needed. But it is not interference by the adult. The parent's control is in the outer boundaries (here, which puzzle); the child's control is in what goes on within that boundary (here, how the puzzle is solved).

For many families, this battle for control shows itself most prominently in how the child's room is maintained. The parents want the room orderly, dirty clothes put where they belong, the bed made, the floor visible. The child often has other ideas.

So what is the outer boundary set by the parent for the child's bedroom? Usually, it is in the choice of which room is given to the child. The child's boundary is the room itself; what goes on within it is his responsibility. Yet if the room is messy or in some way does not quite meet the parent's standards for upkeep, altercations result. Who really is responsible for both setting the standards and for maintaining it? Who has final say? Need the other even be involved when it is one child's room (that is, not shared with siblings)?

Rhiannon had a friend who was notorious for having a messy bedroom. Her parents were not pleased. They tried using any means they could think of to get the girl to clean it up. They would borrow money from their daughter but refuse to pay her back until the room was neat. Sometimes, she could not play with friends until the room was clean. Other times, her allowance would be withheld although it had not been stipulated that an orderly bedroom was a condition for payment.

Many times, the room would remain messy for weeks. The fact that money due her was withheld did not matter. Nor did denial of playtime with friends. But having control over how her room looked and when she would clean it *did* matter to her. Sometimes out of frustration with not having this playmate available, Rhiannon would clean the room for her friend. In short, the parents' methods were ineffective. They did not make their daughter clean the room in a timely fashion. And, as when Rhiannon would do it, sometimes the methods would result in her not cleaning the room at all. Certainly, they never resulted in her *wanting* to make the effort herself.

Years later, Rhiannon made the observation that, among her friends, those who had neat bedrooms were all homeschoolers. Those who had messy rooms were all traditionally schooled. While I do not know if this is true beyond this miniscule sample, I will speculate that the schooling has an influence. I suspect that those children who feel they have control over their lives will tend to have neater rooms. Those who do not feel in control of much in their lives will try to exert control where they can. Keeping a messy room when it is contrary to their parents' wishes is one way to maintain control, however minor. In this small sample, Rhiannon's homeschooled friends all had tremendous control over their education. It was not a life of parents' dictating the assignments for the week. Instead, it was instances of the children deciding what to study.

Whether my speculation is valid or not, when the parent puts the child in charge of his own room, then the decision and responsibility for a neat bedroom rest with the child. This goes back to respecting the child. If we have truly given the child responsibility for his own bedroom, then we respect his desire to maintain it according to his choices. Unless a fire hazard exists or mold is destroying the carpet or emanating odors are offending the rest of the family, the state of the child's bedroom is best determined by the child. Of course, if the state of the room is not up to the child but is decided by the parent, this is another matter. It is then made clear that the parent is in charge of this.

Our level of control matters far more where our child's safety is concerned. But here, too, the question is not "Do we control?" but "How much control should we exert?" And, as with most parenting issues, there is rarely a definitive line. Instead, it depends. It depends upon the child's experience, confidence, skill, and desire; it depends upon our assessment of the child and the situation; and it depends upon our own feelings on the matter.

The issue of control enters as soon as the child is mobile. Most conscientious parents know enough to put hazardous substances out of the reach of their toddlers. It is far simpler than constantly monitoring the child with frequent "no's." And it is far more enjoyable for the child to be able to explore the environment unfettered by barriers or words of warning.

But what is hazardous? It is not so easily agreed upon. In *The Continuum Concept*, Jean Liedloff describes how toddlers of the Yequana (South American Indians) are allowed to crawl and wander about the village. There are large, deep pits, yet the children never fall into them. Knives and machetes are also left lying around. Youngsters periodically pick them up and wave them about, yet here, too, there are no injuries. The same goes for firebrands and open fires. The author describes how babies playing with firebrands not only do not hurt themselves but also they are careful not to touch anyone else or any of the wooden buildings and thatch roofs.

What is dangerous or harmful to us is totally different to the Yequana. And vice versa. This is an extreme example. Even if Western civilization were to adopt the Yequana's methods for infant raising, it would likely still not allow the children to explore unsupervised, areas with huge holes in the ground or sharp knives lying around.

Yet between that extreme of tremendous freedom and the extreme of restriction where the child is given no room to explore, there is a world of circumstances open to disagreement. How much does one control a child? When does one rein him in? How careful an eye and ear does one maintain?

It depends. It depends upon the circumstances, the child's capabilities, the environment, and, mostly, the adult's interpretation of those elements.

At a local library, my young children would while away the last minutes of our stay by playing outside and in front of the building as I checked out our books. Very few people were around on these weekday mornings. Even if patrons would arrive, with steps ten feet wide, the library entrance offered plenty of room for all. What the children most enjoyed was sliding down the handrail. Next on their list was walking along the wall adjacent to the steps. It is about 18 inches wide and, although only a few feet above the steps, it is, in places, about eight feet above the ground along the outer edge. A width of 18 inches is plenty for walking, especially for confident and coordinated children. But not everyone thought so. The library staff asked that the children not walk or climb on the wall. They were afraid the children would get hurt and the library would be liable.

Concerns for liability will always push one back to taking no chances. Better safe than sorry is the motto. But where is one truly safe?

There is, of course, *always* the chance of injury. My son at 13 would turn around in the house and walk into doors. Or he would gesticulate with his arms and hit them against the doorjamb. I remember an elementary schoolmate walking through a glass door, thinking the door was open. Recently in the news was the case of a teenager who was putting away a gun. As he turned to leave, his hand holding the gun hit the wall, and the gun fired and hit his best friend. Who needs to worry about pedophiles or hit-and-run drivers when one can be seriously hurt in one's own home?

The solution is not to bar one from any activity that has even the most remote possibility of danger. It is impossible. There is a risk in everything we do. And that is a key point. If we work to rid all dangers from our children's lives, we must fail. Life is full of risks. We can neither guard against nor possibly anticipate every single one.

A far wiser approach is to teach how to operate in a world of dangers. We cannot imagine every situation that our child could encounter, so the tools we provide must be more general. They include confidence so the child knows he *can* handle this, creativity so he can figure out *how* to handle it, experience so he has reason to be confident. Being put into new and challenging situations allows the child to test himself and to learn more.

When younger, my oldest daughter was in a class of 15, which had a sleepover at the school. This was hardly a novel situation. Almost all of the children had slept at friends' houses on numerous occasions. And all were familiar with the location as well as their fellow participants. Yet some of these third-, fourth-, and fifth-grade students put on quite a show in being separated from their parents. The worst cases were those children who had been told that they could call their parents, and, if they became homesick, the parents would retrieve them. The ultimate was one father who hung on until the very last moment to see if his son would be all right. It was no surprise that the boy went home that evening with his dad. It was, of course, what his father had expected. Why else had he stayed and constantly asked if the boy would prefer to come home? The message – the "correct" answer – was clear.

These parents were giving their children the unmistakable signal that they did not expect the children to feel comfortable spending the night away. It is difficult for a child to feel self-confident when his own parents do not have sufficient confidence in him. When the parents say, essentially, that the child will probably not be able to do it (whether participate in a sleepover away from home or manage any task that is a bit of a challenge), the child's job is doubly hard. He must overcome his own doubts as well as those of his parents – the all-wise ones. A simple "Good-bye. I know you'll do fine. See you tomorrow" would have worked wonders on these children. Instead, they were left confused. They were left wondering why they were there if they were not expected to make it through the night without a rescue by the parents.

Shielding children from all possible danger and pain is another way of chipping away at their self-confidence. It implies that we do not think the children can handle the situation, so they must be kept away from it. "It" is not necessarily danger and pain. "It" is the mere possibility of a hurtful experience. So the fear is that the children cannot handle certain situations or will surely get hurt if they try.

So children walking on an 18-inch ledge might fall and get hurt. The little girl mentioned previously who carried her doll stroller up the stairs could misstep and fall. My children climbing a tree could lose their grip and fall many feet to the ground.

In all of these cases, the children were perfectly capable of coping with the situation at hand. My tree-climbers and ledge-walkers ably demonstrated this. Likewise, the children at the sleepover were emotionally capable of being separated from their parents for a night. They had demonstrated that fact to their parents in sleepovers at friends' homes many times before. The girl with the little stroller was well-coordinated and physically capable of the challenge before her. For the children at the sleepover and the little girl, all that was lacking was the adult's or parent's acknowledgement of that capability: "Yes, you can do that."

Take this scenario forward several years. Rather than young children, they are now teenagers and adults. At this point, do we still want them to hold back in fear or to wait for another's approval before venturing into the unknown or different or challenging? Would we want the person not to give a speech because he might make mistakes and be emotionally hurt and embarrassed? Would we prefer the athlete not to try a triple spin on the ice skates because he might slip, fall, and be injured? Would we want the college graduate not to pursue his dream because he could fail and lose everything?

We are naturally empathic creatures. Even infants who hear another cry in pain will join in although they are not themselves hurting. A parent's natural reaction to her child's suffering is also empathy. Likewise, a parent's inclination is to protect her dear one from harm. What kind of person would purposely do otherwise and force her child to endure pain? No normal parent would intentionally inflict pain on her child solely to let him learn to deal with it.

Yet pain is a natural part of life. It is unavoidable. We can lessen the likelihood of the child encountering pain. But probably more important than helping the child avoid what is hurtful is teaching the child how to deal with suffering. Excruciatingly painful circumstances need not be sought out. Minor mishaps can just as readily do the job, and they happen all of the time.

Scraped knees are all too common for young children just gaining competence in upright mobility. When a tumble happens in front of the parent, a familiar scene unfolds. The child invariably looks to the parent for cues. Should he cry or not? A parent who fusses over the accident will draw out cries even from the most minor of incidents. A parent who makes no big deal of one more fall and scrape will elicit a different response: the child gets up and carries on. This child learns how to handle pain. He sees that minor injuries can be ignored and will not interfere with the activity.

However the parent reacts and however the child, in turn, reacts, control is an issue here. In the first case, the fussing parent retains control. Or rather, control remains external to the child. So it is a sympathetic word or a kiss or, better, a fancy Band-Aid© that will make the pain go away. In contrast, in the second case, the child is the one in control. He decides if the pain is great enough to generate cries. He decides if the injury is minor enough not to interfere with continued play. A Band-Aid© may stop the bleeding, but it is not necessary to stop the pain. That power comes from within him.

I learned that lesson firsthand when I was seven years old. A door had been slammed shut on my finger. A mere thread of skin held the slammed end to the rest of the joint. As I sat waiting in the emergency room, my parents spoke to the staff and filled out medical and insurance forms. Meanwhile, the policeman who had escorted my speeding father to the hospital tried to console me. Eventually, above my cries, his words came through. "It didn't hurt that much." I could stop crying, he told me, if I wanted.

Indeed, the floodgates had been open long enough. I was getting the attention and was about to get the care I needed. Crying certainly was not helping the situation at that point. So I stopped. And it was okay. It was tremendous feeling that I have remembered always. I was, then, the one in control. I did not have to cry. And I could control the pain. It really was not as bad as my screams had made out.

Such an accident is not to be wished upon anyone. A normal parent would never purposely subject her child to pain or unnecessarily prolong a painful experience. Yet most children seem to encounter some such accidents, even under the best of circumstances. One of my daughters cut her tongue when lifting her bike up a few short steps. The bump of a flap of skin on her tongue remains to this day. Another daughter fractured her arm roller-skating at a rink. My son's appendix ruptured. And so it goes.

All have had numerous opportunities to experience different levels of pain. Having learned when they were young how to react to minor accidents, the children were better able to cope when more serious incidents occurred. They realized that there was no point to heeding cuts and scrapes. Making a fuss about such only interrupted play. Better, they could control the pain themselves – by ignoring it as they continued play. To run to an adult for sympathy put the control in the adult's hands and was no better with eliminating the pain.

My children's job, then, became one of distinguishing what different types of pain meant. Was it minor and could be ignored? Was it minor but needed minimal care, such as a BandAid© to check the bleeding? Or was it severe and required adult assistance?

Pain is a natural response of our body to harm done to it. With experience, we learn when and how to respond in turn to this natural reaction. It is an ongoing process as new hurts are felt and analyzed. Sometimes the learning takes longer for some of us. At 11, my son still found it difficult to tell when his stomach hurt because he was hungry, was sick with the flu, had eaten too much candy, or had to use the toilet. At 14, he can finally make these distinctions.

The more the child can handle himself, the more confident and capable he will become. But initially, at least, he looks to his parents for guidance. Through their example and words, they let the child know what to do under which circumstances. Minor scrapes can be ignored; they are not important. Bleeding that will not stop can often be taken care of by the child. Pain that continues and intensifies needs help from others.

Pain control does not mean ignoring all pain. It means, instead, learning what to ignore, what to heed, and how to react.

A similar pattern emerges when the child tries something new or challenging. Unsure of himself, he often looks to the parent. Is it okay to try? Is he capable of accomplishing the feat or, at least, safely attempting it? Can he do it on his own?

So back to those ledges at the library. A child who is afraid and sees that fear reflected in his parent will not do well. He reads in his parent's eyes that he might not be able to walk that without falling. He takes on his parent's fear – or possible expectation – and does not even make the attempt. Or worse, he tries and fails, thus confirming his and his parent's worst fears.

A friend illustrated the effect of a parent's lack of confidence and the power of suggestion. The girl was chopping wood with only sandals on her feet. She had been at it without mishap for some time. Then her father noticed her feet and told her she would hit her bare foot if she did not change footwear. Her next swipe of the axe – you guessed it – hit her toe.

Equally damaging is the parent who pushes the child not just beyond his comfort zone but into areas beyond his capability. The child is bound to fail or get hurt in his attempt to satisfy the parent. For, indeed, it is the parent's ego at work here. Whether it is to make the parent proud of what the child can do or to fulfill unmet aspirations of the parent, they are the needs or desires of the *parent* that are behind the child's actions.

Between these two extremes of fear of even trying and pushing to achieve for the parent is an ideal middle ground. We want the child to be the one to assess the situation in terms of what he knows he can do. This is based on experience. Has he done this before? Was he successful? Is he more capable now? Has he done something similar? How different is it? What is the risk – a short tumble to soft ground or a life-threatening pitch down a sheer cliff? If our confidence enters into the picture, it is to confirm what the child already feels. So, if the child believes he can do it, we, too, believe.

Ultimately, it is our understanding of the child based upon trust and respect that determines where this middle ground lies. We trust that he will choose experiences based upon his capabilities. We respect his choices. We understand, then, why he chooses as he does. It is not to please us. It is not to give in to our fears. It is not to prove something to the world. It is simply because he believes he can, because he has pleasure in the doing, because he finds joy in testing his capabilities.

This discussion does not apply, of course, to self-destructive acts, more often undertaken by older children. A supportive parent does not allow or even encourage alcoholic consumption by minors, driving when drunk, engaging in promiscuity, or other illegal or inappropriate activities. When a child engages in such acts, he is not looking for parental approval. He may be seeking peer approval. He may be trying to escape problems at home. He may be crying for help. But the last thing he needs is support for his misguided actions.

. Our support is not meant to boost the child's ego. Our job is not to inflate it. We want a child on an even keel – one who knows what he can do, one who feels confident in taking on new tasks that slightly stretch his limits, one who has no problem in *not* doing other tasks that he feels are beyond him. He feels no shame in the latter just as he is not compelled to brag about the former. It is just a comfortable feeling knowing that he can do some things, cannot do others, and is growing in his ability to do more.

The parent's role parallels this. She no more shames the child because of what he cannot do than she makes a big deal of what he can do.

This idea runs counter to what many would have us do for the child. And it runs counter to what many themselves do for children. It is as if children have such fragile egos that we parents must always be boosting them. If anything, excessive praise may well cause the child to question his ability. That is, if he is doing so well, why must the adults go to such lengths to recognize it?

Positive praise has other negative effects, as well. Robert E. Bills, in *Education for Intelligence*, explains this well:

> But even positive evaluation is threatening, forcing the locus of responsibility to become external. When other people evaluate us positively, they imply that they have a right to evaluate. This in turn implies that negative evaluations of our behavior will be forthcoming if they do not approve... (199)

This is so true. When Rhiannon was 12 and Rikki, 10, I talked to them about adults evaluating them. Did they find that criticism encourages them to do better or that it demoralizes them? Rhiannon said it made her feel bad. Rikki countered that such comments did make her want to improve, but she really preferred to have neither criticism nor compliment.

Rikki, in at least one respect in this matter, was similar to many other children I have observed. When working on a project and approached by an adult, she would cover up her work. It was not that she was ashamed of her work. Instead, she wished to ward off the possibility of any comments. As Bills indicates, if one is allowed to compliment, then one also has the right to criticize.

Son Ty, years earlier, had demonstrated to me how such evaluations felt. Ty was three and busy working on a difficult project. He seemed to be doing a good job. To encourage his efforts, I said, "Yes" and then, "That's right." But it was too much for him. "Mommy, don't talk," was his response.

Later the same day, I was trying to extricate a newly purchased lawn mower from its box. As I struggled, Ty encouraged me with "Good. That's right. That's right."

Far from being bolstered by his comments, I felt insulted and annoyed. I knew quite well that I was doing the right thing; after all, the mower *was* coming out, however slowly. His comments were not necessary, not appreciated, and not helpful. But they were effective in showing me how such evaluations are often received by children.

If positive comments are not appreciated, imagine how the negative ones are received. Even Rikki, who claimed they gave her impetus to do better, did not want them given in the first place. Indeed, several years earlier when only eight, Rikki had been adamant about having absolutely no judgments about her or her work. Criticisms were out of the question. It is more, I believe, the idea of constant evaluation that is so annoying. The child's every move is under scrutiny. Did he do right? Or did he commit another blunder?

This, too, I experienced firsthand. I was at a local park throwing a toy for our dog to retrieve. A fellow dog owner commented on how I threw "just like a girl." As I continued to throw the toy, he continued to throw out his unsolicited jibes. It was most irritating. The man's comments were obviously rude. But more than that, I had a sense of how children must feel under constant evaluation by adults. Like them, I felt my every move was under scrutiny. Thanks to this fellow's comments, I became more and more aware of every toss of the toy. I knew that my dog, the one for whom my throws were intended, was pleased just with the fact that I was throwing his toy. Yet I could not place that idea above the commentary. I began wondering, too, where it would end. My simple throwing of a toy elicited negative comments. How about other mundane actions on my part? I probably stand "just like a girl," probably talk "just like a girl." Would those, too, bring on unwanted remarks?

At least for me, such evaluations could be avoided by timing my visits to the park to later in the day. But for children under the eye of their parents or teacher or other well-meaning adults, there is often no avoidance of evaluation. Adults are everywhere with their comments. "Don't do this" and "stop doing that"; "keep up the good work" and "great job." For them, too, where does it end? When can they relax and just be?

At home, we would hope. Outside the home, well-intentioned adults will continue to offer their opinions. At home and with us, at least, our children can have a safe haven. When they want evaluations, they will ask us. This is simple respect. We treat them as we ourselves wish to be treated – without evaluation and with acceptance. In the meantime, we can offer them better alternatives. One is our acceptance of them as they are. Another is shared emotions. When they are disappointed, we can feel their sadness, too. When they are pleased, we can feel pleasure with them. Pride and joy in a job well done can be happily shared.

Finally, we can express our gratitude for what they have done. A simple "thank you" works wonders. Even when it is given for the child doing what he should do (as in an assigned chore or a requested task), it is well received. And it does double duty. First, it acknowledges the child's action. Second, it shows appreciation for that action. As mentioned earlier, everyone wants respect. That respect is intimately tied to being recognized for who one is, for what one does. Saying "thank you" is one way of showing respect.

I must add that this thanking is genuine and not manipulative. That is, it is not said before the child completes the task in order to persuade him to do it. It is, instead, heartfelt gratitude for what has been done. It is likely to be a simple task (e.g., remembering to take out the garbage), but it is the smooth workings of those little things that make for a pleasant life with others.

Without a doubt, it is pleasant to be around those who are grateful. Further, one wants to do more to please such people. I speak both as the giver of such gratitude, as well as the receiver.

At one point, my daughter Rhiannon made an effort of thanking me for what I did for her, even for rather minor efforts of typical parent jobs, such as chauffeuring. The first time that she did this, I was taken aback. I was both pleased and surprised. As it went on, I continued to enjoy her acknowledging my efforts for her.

It is easy to forget such niceties when among family. Yet for whom do we care more than our own family members? Should not they be among the first to receive our expressions of thanks?

There is probably no method as powerful in affecting our children's behavior as the example we set. Good or bad, our children learn best from what we do. Expressing thanks for their efforts is just one of a myriad of ways we can teach our children by example.

It works both ways. We have no better reflection of how we appear to others than in the behavior of our children. While each of us comes with his or her own personality, our actions, behavior, and interactions with others are closely tied to what we have learned from our family. When we see something done by our child that we do not like, we pause and ask, "Is this something I have taught by my own actions?" Such instances, then, become opportunities for two to improve. When we change our behavior for the better, we also set the stage for our children improving. Put another way, how can we expect proper behavior from our children if we ourselves do not practice it?

Observing one's own children with these points in mind becomes a most humbling experience. Once when hearing one of my children respond impatiently to playmates in a game, I realized my own impatience with the children. When hearing another be especially critical of friends, I understood why it disturbed me so. It was too close to home, a reflection of my own failing. Not only was I seeing myself as one who criticizes too readily, I was also seeing how I had taught my daughter to do the same all too well.

There have been times I have wished other parents, also, were more aware of this.

Our city neighborhood is a good one. Children are often outside playing or running to friends' homes. Unfortunately, not all adults would receive neighbor children's knocks on the door with consideration. One in particular would barely open the front door before saying that the child inside could not play. There was not even a chance for the door-knocking child to *ask* for the friend. And, sometimes, playing with that neighbor child was not even the reason for the visit. It did not take long for this neighbor's young children to respond in a like way to potential playmates. Where before the children would welcome visiting neighbors and be glad to have others to play with, they soon were responding as the parent had. The door would barely open and "We don't want to play" would greet the children. It was so sad seeing the rudeness of the parent echoed in the children.

While setting a good example is the most effective way of teaching proper behavior, it can be the hardest for the parent. We are, alas, not perfect. But to give the good example, we must first reform ourselves. This is after having lived for decades with our present personalities and behaviors. The years have been spent not so much in improving our personal characteristics as in learning how to live with them, good or bad, or in ensuring they are solidly entrenched within us. Now, to be made aware of our faults through the mirroring of our children presents us with a most difficult task.

It is far easier to correct our child's transgressions than to work on ours. It is far easier to pull the power play: we as the parents in charge command the lowly child to do right while we ignore our own failings. Our faults are, after all, well ingrained after years of practice. It would be much harder for us to reform.

Indeed, it is. But that is hardly justification for ignoring what we should do.

Raising children is one of the most life-expanding experiences there is. It is not just the lifelong commitment one makes to one's child. For children cannot be divorced; they are forever. It is not just seeing life once again from a child's point of view. The world is fresh and wondrous and full of opportunities when with them. It is not just seeing life from our parents' point of view. We now understand what our own parents went through with raising us.

It is also seeing ourselves through the clear and honest eyes of our children. Leaving ourselves open to this view, one that shows us as we really are, gives us a tremendous opportunity. With our children we, too, can grow and become a better person. That is the true challenge, the difficult path.

Or we can choose the easy way. We can pretend that we are perfect, that we know everything, that we are all-powerful. We can never admit to mistakes. We can forbid our children from questioning our actions. We can force our children to obey us. This all we can do because we are in charge.

But in the end we, parent and child, both lose. Such a parent gets obedience, but not respect. Rebellion, anger, and pain rest uneasily just below the surface. Such a parent has compliance but not cooperation. The child works *for* the parent, not with her. Such a parent teaches the child to do the same with his own children. The cycle continues and the opportunity for growth remains elusive.

Unless . . . . Or until. . . .

One does learn from example, good or bad. Children are sponges soaking up what is given them. But they do not remain so forever. They grow into adults and then can finally ask, "Is this right?" We are now these children-become-adults, and we can at last honestly answer: "No, it is not right to pretend to be right when we are not. No, it is not right to pretend to be perfect when we are not. And, no, it is not right to reform our children while ignoring our own need to reform." We can break that cycle. We can take control. Instead of feeling powerful because of what we can make others, our children, do, we can feel powerful because of what we can do to ourselves: reform. In this is great satisfaction. We improve ourselves and set the stage for our children becoming those good people we want them to be.

Our parental role can then be simply stated, if not so simply accomplished. First, we understand our children. From this we create an environment where they can learn, explore, and flourish. We support them in their endeavors. We are grateful for their help. And, most important, we always set the good example.

Chapter 10

The Experts

I was my mother's darling child,
Brought up with care and trouble.
For fear a spoon would hurt my mouth,
She fed me with a shovel.

The danger for the parent, whether taking the stance of the all-powerful one or the one working with the child, is to discredit one's own ability to raise her child. The tendency is to turn to experts for advice.

Parents have been successfully raising their children for eons. What defines success? At the least, it is having children grow into adults who continue their society. They contribute to their community's life through their role – parent, healer, leader, etc. They carry on traditions that give meaning to the communal life.

If parents in ages past had not been successful, we would not be here today. What has happened that parents no longer know how to raise their children but must now turn to experts with credentials?

It is not so much that we do not know, for much of this knowledge is innate. It is more that we parents have been led to believe we do not know. The focus on science, on years of education, on controlled studies has resulted in the elevation of the expert in child raising. It is no longer the parent who is the expert from having spent hours with her child. It is the degreed behaviorist or psychologist or educator who knows best. After all, such have spent years reading other experts' works, have conducted studies to discover which methods work best, and have received a degree, no less, which proves they know best.

And sometimes they do. Other times they do not. And if the parent has the belief that these experts always know best, she will not distinguish between those who know and those who do not. Nor will she even be aware that they can be wrong.

Although the experts do have years of education and a wealth of scientific studies behind them, there is something they do not have that *we* do, and it is most important: an intimate knowledge of our own child. All the scientific studies cannot know our individual child. The studies show, at best, tendencies – what most children do under the given constraints. They are often done in artificial or contrived circumstances, ones that may not be relevant to real-life experiences. Studies often look at a part of the whole and expect results to apply to that part when it is once again seen within the whole.

Worse, expecting what is true of a person some of the time to be true of the person all of the time leads to applying labels. We generalize, categorize, and segment by certain characteristics. Scientists especially love to group similar items, attributes, people, or whatever together. This is handy when wanting, for instance, to identify a certain bird. Grouping living creatures by species and genus makes such identification possible. Naming them makes identification understandable to all.

But categorizing a person is not always so beneficial. As Soren Kierkegaard said, "Once you label me, you negate me." The whole person – all of his attributes, characteristics, personality, potential – gives way to the label. He is buried under the defining aspects of that one word; everything else about him is forgotten. So, for instance, for the child labeled hyperactive, any energetic display is seen as supportive of the label. That all children have a need to use their energy in physically active ways is ignored. Forgotten, too, are the times when the child is quiet. Such behavior does not support the label, so it is ignored.

Prejudice is not confined to the races or genders or age groups. It happens all of the time. And it is not just imposed by others. Individuals just as readily label themselves. I recall a coworker who, after transposing two numbers, excused her mistake. She was, she said, math dyslexic. It is a common error for a person to mix up digits when recalling numbers. Who has not done it? Yet most of us would not label ourselves dyslexic because of such a mistake. This woman did, and in so doing, she negated herself as well as if an outsider had categorized her. With such a label, she was, then, free to continue to make such mistakes. After all, it is expected of one with math dyslexia. Worse, by so defining herself, she was leaving no room for the possibility of correcting her problem. She was, she believed, math dyslexic and that was that.

Seeing only a part of the child has been an unfortunate aspect of our educational system. For most of the twentieth century, schools have emphasized achievement in mathematics and linguistics (reading, writing, spelling). Then in 1983, along came Howard Gardner and his *Frames of Mind: The Theory of Multiple Intelligences.* He presented his belief that children are not only either math proficient or language proficient. They can be capable in five other areas as well. This was great for those who fell into these newly "discovered" categories. Now they, too, could be seen by teachers, parents, and other adults as successes as they pursued their areas of interest. As liberating as it was for such children, such pronouncements were no better than those before, which defined success in school only in terms of math or linguistic proficiency. In both cases, success or even acceptability was limited only to some areas of expertise. What of those children who fell outside these categories? Because they do not fit inside these parameters, are they not successful, not acceptable, or not achieving?

Not surprisingly, several years after these new categories of "intelligence" were presented, three others were "discovered." (They are detailed in Howard Gardner's *Intelligence Reframed.*) Again, this is wonderful for those children who now have an acceptable academic specialty. But, once more, this still does not help those who remain outside the named categories.

The point is, why must we categorize children so? Why do we describe successful children as only those who fit within a few specified areas of interest? Why limit them? Is this not disrespectful to downgrade a child's interest because it is not one of the chosen ones? Why need we let others, the so-called experts, define success for our children?

Another problem with experiments of children is that the study itself affects the outcome. (This is similar to what happens when we get our blood pressure checked in a doctor's office. The stress of being there often causes us to have a higher reading than we would otherwise.) Scientists are well aware of the fact that their presence can alter the reactions of the participants. Removing a child from his natural environment to observe him is enough to skew results. Add a stranger to the mix, and the findings may be further from what would occur under natural conditions. John Holt, in *How Children Learn*, describes one such experiment. In order to discover where children's eyes move when looking at an object, the subjects' heads had to be secured. That is, the experimenters wanted only the eyes to move, not the whole head. Not surprisingly, most children balked when they saw the scary looking device that was to clamp down and hold their head in place. For those few willing to subject themselves to this treatment, one can only wonder how natural were their eye movements.

Since they are aware that the observer can affect the behavior of the one studied, most scientists work to have a natural setting. So they may watch the child through one-way mirrors so their presence is not evident. Or the researchers may go to the child's home. Yet these situations are still not how it normally is for the child. The environment is different, and we cannot be sure in what way those changes affect the observed outcomes.

It is not surprising that some of the most insightful observations of children come from people who were not conducting scientific experiments but were lay people just observing children. Some of these observers have written down what they saw to share with others. So we have Alison Stallibrass (*The Self-Respecting Child: Development Through Spontaneous Play*), John Holt, Frances Wickes (*The Inner World of Childhood*), and A. S. Neill (*The Dominie Books of A.S. Neill*), among others.

In reading the works of such authors, we clearly see how we, too, can learn from watching our children. We do not need special training or an advanced degree. But we do need to be open to seeing what is really happening. And we need to be nonintrusive in our observing.

We also need to be respectful of the child. That is, we treat him as a human being who has feelings and needs and natural reactions. He is not merely a thing, a component in an experiment, or a pawn for scientific manipulation. He is a person, and we care about him. That is foremost in our minds as we observe him.

This is not to say experts and their research have no value. Rather, it says results and words of advice need to be received with caution. One would go crazy and certainly be no better off if one were to read every publication on child raising. Each one has a special focus, is based on only so many studies, and offers its unique methods. There is, of course, some overlap in ideas presented. But there are also divergent views.

Worse, if the result of so much advice is to undermine a parent's self-confidence in raising her child, such advice does great harm. A child picks up on this, so neither parent nor child is well-served.

It is not unusual to read a book and try its method on our children. Then when it does not work – we do not apply the method quite right or we are too tired to be consistent or we do not know exactly what this specific situation calls for – we abandon that method. We soon move on to another, give it a try, fail, then cast that one aside, too. So it goes. But the problems remain. Added to them now is our confusion. Why will nothing work? What is wrong with us or with our child? Where is the solution? The confusion is not less for the children subjected to experiment after experiment.

In contrast, a parent who has spent the time observing her child is far better off. She knows her child, understands why he acts in certain ways under different circumstances. She sees him not as a statistic but as a unique individual. And, most important, she has his best interests in mind. The others often have hidden agendas. If nothing else, the experts want to be seen as right. Each has methods and beliefs based on his or her perception of what is wrong and how best to fix the situation. They are the experts. They are supposed to know. To admit otherwise is to weaken their position.

This frequently comes up in school where the teacher and text are always correct. This can reach a level of absurdity. For example, in daughter Rikki's driver's education course, the students learned of some laws that had recently been changed. The students were taught the law both as it used to be as well as how it is now. For the state exam, they were expected, quite naturally, to know the current law. But for the class, they were expected to give answers on the test based upon the old law. The course tests were set up based upon the old law and rather than, for instance, eliminate that question or manually mark it, the students were to give what was essentially the wrong answer. That is, the teacher's guide was correct and not to be questioned.

Examples of the experts being wrong are all around us. For instance, in a book I read, the author was trying to show how her daughter's teacher helped the child figure out the correct answer after giving a wrong one. The exercise was to discover through experimentation which of several items float and which ones sink. The girl had written that crayons float. It was the wrong answer so the teacher wrote, "Try again." What child does not know that that really means "wrong"? If "float" is wrong, then "sink" must be correct. Why bother trying the experiment again? But here is the real catch. How can a child not tell a crayon has sunk? Who would confuse floating for sinking? It did not make sense to me. So I conducted my own experiment. Lo and behold, I found that among my children's crayons some float and some sink. The teacher and her guide were wrong. They were likely based on one crayon test. What is a child to think? Here is her experience, at odds with the teacher's answer. But the teacher, the expert, is right.

Then there is the well-known child development authority, Jean Piaget. Through his studies, Piaget discovered that children's minds develop in an orderly fashion. For instance, a two-month-old infant has no concept of otherness; he and his mother are one. Only months later does he understand his mother's separateness, and only then does he become upset when she leaves him.

Piaget's studies showed that because of this sequential mental development, children were able to understand certain concepts only at specific ages. But we have previously noted how observations by John Holt, among others, found Piaget's theories not always to be true. (Remember the girl blowing the balloon across the floor, for example.) It must be noted that Piaget's work was with a limited group of children and at a specific era. What can we say of children now? Do children learn concepts more quickly? Does a different environment affect mental development? What of children of other cultures, subjected to far different child care methods? We have seen how "normal" behavior in American children is not so in all cultures. Is this so with Piaget's theories of the mental development of children?

Experts, even revered ones such as Piaget, are not infallible. They draw conclusions based upon observations made at a specific time, under limiting conditions, with a selected group of children. Those parameters may be irrelevant for conclusions about our own child. It would be a mistake to believe that all such scientific studies' results apply to all children.

Mistakes about the stages and timing of a child's mental development may not have a great bearing on our child's life. But it is important to realize the broader issue that experts are not always right. Unfortunately, sometimes when they are wrong, they are terribly wrong.

Expert advice is not always in the form of action. Sometimes it says, "Do nothing" or "There is nothing wrong" despite parents' belief that there is, indeed, something not right. Liz Birt and Maurice Lopez entitle their tale "Don't Give Up: Matthew's Story" (*Mothering*, #100, May/June 2000: 53). Their autistic toddler had various complaints. Among others, his stomach hurt, he could not sleep regularly, and he had chronic diarrhea. The doctors at well-known Chicago hospitals could find nothing wrong and felt psychiatric care was called for. As the title indicates, the parents trusted their son over the experts. Something was obviously very wrong, and it was not in the boy's head. It was only with contact with a doctor in England and a routine x-ray that the cause of the little boy's suffering was discovered. His colon was impacted by fecal matter the size of a small cantaloupe!

Listening to the experts can do more than cause years of unnecessary suffering. Taking their word as gospel can result in radically, negatively, and permanently altering a child's life. Some operations, once performed, cannot be undone.

Hear the story of a nine-year-old boy as described by Peter Schrag and Diane Divoky in *The Myth of the Hyperactive Child & Other Means of Child Control.* "J. M." had seizures and behavior problems, including hyperactivity, aggression, destruction, and sadism. The cure was brain surgery. Left and right thalamotomies were performed. One of these was repeated nine months later. Behavior seemed to improve, but a year later the same problems reappeared. So surgery in a different area of the brain was performed. The result was impaired memory and increased behavior problems. One month later, a simultaneous bilateral thalamotomy was done with supposedly marked behavior improvement.

The surgeon, Orlando J. Andy, performed about 14 such operations on children as young as six between 1961 and 1974. Most patients were supposedly hyperactive, aggressive, or maladjusted. Andy had varying degrees of success. "Poor" was the outcome of a 14-year-old who died a few weeks after the operation. J. M., preceding, was luckier. His results were termed "good" despite Andy describing the boy's intellectual capacity as "deteriorating."

Less extreme, yet no less shocking, is the description of Farrall Instrument Company's AR-5 Receiver-Shocker and Transmitter for remote wireless shocking of humans. According to company president William Farrell, more than 100 schools and other institutions were using the devices, although not in regular classrooms.

This was more than 25 years ago. We may smugly claim that such methods were rare and are no longer even used today. Indeed, it may be true that children are not given electrical shocks to alter their behavior. But that is not to say other, equally harmful means are not at the experts' disposal.

Devastating in its own right is what is done now to "help" children. The diagnosis of attention-deficit hyperactive disorder (ADHD) and its cousins, attention-deficit disorder (ADD), minimal brain dysfunction, hyperactivity, etc., is rampant in our country. Estimates of those with this "disorder" range from 10 to 25 percent of children in school. While brain surgery is no longer the ultimate cure, the current common remedy can be, nonetheless, still life-altering in a negative way.

The most common solution for an ADHD diagnosis is drugs, and the most commonly prescribed drug is Ritalin. Several sources, including *Running on Ritalin: A Physician Reflects on Children, Society, and Performance in a Pill* by Lawrence H. Diller, *What to Look for in a Classroom and Other Essays* by Alfie Kohn, and especially, *Talking Back to Ritalin: What Doctors Aren't Telling You About Stimulants and ADHD* by Peter R. Breggin, cite sobering statistics on this increasingly popular drug. For instance, in 1997, more than five million people, most of them children, were prescribed Ritalin, an increase of 700 percent since 1990. These ADHD drugs are often taken for long periods, for years, sometimes even into adulthood. This is despite the fact that these drugs are intended for short-term use only. On the other hand, it is no wonder that long-term use is not uncommon since these drugs are addictive. Drugs are given even though their effects vary tremendously from child to child, from exacerbating the problem to having no change in behavior to dulling the activity level. Drugs continue to be prescribed even though there are dangerous side effects. For instance, Ritalin, the drug of choice, is the trade name for methylphenidate. It is a mild central nervous system stimulant. Because it is an amphetamine-like drug, it can be habit forming, leading to marked tolerance and serious physical and psychological dependence. *The Medical Advisor: The Complete Guide to Alternative and Conventional Treatments* lists Ritalin's side effects. Less serious ones include "nervousness, trouble sleeping, loss of appetite, headache, dizziness, nausea, stomach pains." The serious side effects include "severe skin rash or hives, irregular or fast heartbeat, chest pain, unusual bruising, blurred vision, joint pain, sore throat and fever, weight loss, mood or mental changes, abnormal behavior patterns, psychotic reactions." And this is supposed to help children behave in school?

One must wonder which is worse, the supposed ADHD problem or its supposed cure. In fact, Peter R. Breggin in *Talking Back to Ritalin* notes that it is not unusual to have referred to him a child who is on as many as four different drugs, each one prescribed to alleviate the adverse side effects of the previously prescribed one. It is no surprise that studies have found children prefer not taking Ritalin. Further, such children as adults say that the drugs taken were more of a hindrance than a help.

So successful has the drug industry been in selling this stimulant that it is now focusing on a new market: children under the age of six. Sadly, one almost expects the drug manufacturers to operate in this way. After all, their goal is the highest rate of return possible, or to put it more crudely, profits before people. What is more distressing is the behavior of those who are supposed to have the child's best interests at

heart – their doctors and teachers. Yet ADHD diagnosis and its popular drug cure continue to be pushed by the medical profession, school
officials, and even parents. This ADHD diagnosis is frequently given
despite there being no consensus on what constitutes ADHD as it is
applied today. In fact, studies have demonstrated that the diagnosis of
the same individual varies wildly among the so-called experts. And the
popularity of the drug cure is firmly entrenched despite the fact that,
according to Breggin, "a consensus will be found among researchers
that stimulant drugs are of no long-term help to children in any aspect
of their lives."

It is too easy for the parent to be intimidated by those who are
expected to be authorities on the subject. Instead, a healthy dose of
skepticism greatly aids the parent. For instance, if the child truly has
ADHD, does he show signs of it all of the time? Or does it happen
only in school or only in certain situations? Does the child spend
extended periods of time on projects at home? (This does not include
watching television or playing computer games.) Could it be there is
something wrong with the environment (most likely, the school) rather
than with the child?

Indeed, those who have disagreed with the ADHD diagnosis have
found much better solutions over drugs. In such instances, the children have been truly listened to. When the child's behavior is obviously extreme or abnormal, as opposed to, say, just fidgety, these adults
have seen that behavior for what it is. Rather than a problem in itself,
it is a manifestation of some other problem. For instance, in the little
gem of a book *No More Ritalin: Treating ADHD Without Drugs*, author
Dr. Mary Ann Block explains how different physical or environmental
problems can mistakenly lead to an ADHD diagnosis. She has found
that allergies and hypoglycemia (low levels of sugar in the blood) often
contribute to such diagnoses.

More likely causes are those that are harder for the parents to deal
with. As Breggin explains, many times a so-called hyperactive child is
merely responding appropriately to his environment. It is his best way
to indicate that, for instance, his class situation is boring, he is not getting appropriate attention from a parent, or his home life does not fully
meet his needs in some other way. Regardless of the reasons for the

hyperactive label, once the true cause of the child's problem is addressed, the "ADHD" symptoms disappear.

Treating the "ADHD" symptoms as if they were the cause is like treating children's bedwetting as if it were the problem. Under such circumstances, the symptoms may go away. But since the underlying cause is not addressed, the real problem remains. At most, it is masked. By not attending to what is behind those symptoms, the problem will continue to manifest itself and eventually find some way to get our attention

It is so important to take the time to truly listen to our children. What are they really saying? Words are not their only form of communication. What they do or do not do is often their way of "speaking" to us. Unnatural, wild behavior is not necessarily due to willful or undisciplined children. Often this is a cry for help by the child, and the last thing he needs is a drug that is supposed to cover up his appeals to us.

While we listen to our child, we also must deal with the teachers, doctors, and others pushing for ADHD diagnosis and treatment. When one is dealing with experts, it is important to remember what their hidden agendas are. Who benefits when a child is diagnosed with ADHD? Who gains when Ritalin is prescribed as the solution? Clearly the drug manufacturer gains with increased sales. Physicians and academicians involved in ADHD research gain by giving credence to their claim that there really is an ADHD problem. For them, more funding of research is called for to understand and properly deal with this problem. Doctors gain with treating one more patient. All of these gain whether the child is helped or not. Ritalin is still sold, another ADHD diagnosis is still made, the doctor's bill is still paid.

Teachers benefit also. A teacher's job is to teach a classroom of children. If some of those children are, by her definition, a problem (whether disruptive or just fidgety), she will naturally want those problems taken care of so she can effectively teach. If drugs quiet the children and give her a more orderly class, such a solution will be easier for her. She need not change her methods of teaching or question the curriculum. The material may be too boring or too advanced or irrelevant or confusing. But if the students will all behave, that good conduct will compensate for poor methods or material. Drugs for active children in her classroom may well be the best solution for her situation. But is it best for your child if he is one of the drugged ones?

In such a situation, the child is helpless. He cannot realistically refuse to take the drug if that is the agreed-upon remedy. He can complain of side effects, but where is the guarantee that anything will be done about it? If there is a problem with the curriculum, who is he to question it? Who can the child turn to for help?

There are only his parents. No others have his best interests in the forefront. He relies upon his parents to question the authorities, to see if his complaints merit investigation, to discover what is at the heart of his problems. And he needs them to take action to help him. This is so for any problem. It may be school authorities pressing for drugs to quiet a restless student. Or it may be simply a teacher who does not correctly interpret a student's behavior.

When my oldest daughter was in first grade, she received a mediocre grade in math for the first term. When I questioned her teacher on it, he explained that she took a long time to do the class math exercises. When I countered that she knew the material, that she had mastered it in kindergarten (at another school), that she was very bright, he was unyielding. "All parents believe their children are bright" was his reply. Well, I surely hope so! Unfortunately, the teacher did not correctly assess the situation. In talking to Rhiannon, I learned that she was bored to tears with material she already knew. She saw no reason to quickly do the math. The "reward" for anyone finishing early was to do more (boring) math problems. If anything, she had incentive not to finish quickly.

That was in January. In the fall, Rhiannon was in a new school where her intelligence was challenged.

Another student from this same small school was also placed in a different school the following fall because the parents were dissatisfied. In this small class of 17, a third child's parent was also dissatisfied with the school, but chose to take no action. She explained that likely no school would ever satisfy them. Rather than search for one that might, she had decided just to make do with the present one.

There is something to be said for consistency. Constantly changing schools in the search for the perfect one does not serve the child well. Yet it is possible, expected even, that one can learn from one's mistakes. One has, as in this case, a clearer idea of what is important in the classroom and what one's own child especially needs. But more, a child knows when the parent is fighting for him. It makes a tremendous difference to the child when he sees that his mother or father not only listens to him and understands him and his problem but also will go the extra mile for him. He is no longer alone in his struggle. He has someone who cares. He has one who can stand up to, question, even, these authority figures.

Some battles children must take on themselves. They will not always have parents nearby to intervene for them. But there are also those battles that, alone, would be senseless to fight; defeat would be inevitable. What child could question an ADHD diagnosis? What child could explain that he really is smart and be believed by his teacher who has her own reasons for thinking otherwise? What child could complain that a subject is boring and expect the teacher to do something about it?

It is not just that the child needs someone to face the adult experts for him. He also needs that someone to interpret what is happening. Rhiannon never told me that the reason she got a mediocre grade in math was because she did the exercises slowly and that was because she was bored. I had to get information from her, then from the teacher, then again from her. (What do you do in math class? Is it easy or hard? Have you done it before? Do you know the material? Why do you take so long?) It means examining the problem from many angles, including the experts' viewpoints. Often this entails a level of understanding that the child does not possess. Young children are limited in their ability to self-analyze. And most have been taught to obey and not contradict the teacher (or any other authority). Such is hardly the background needed by a child to question or take on the experts.

Of course, parents, all of us, are taught to respect the opinions and decisions of authorities. This is so for good reason. The experts do know more than we do about their areas of specialty. They can and do help us. Nor does it make sense to question every single edict that we encounter. That would become tiresome, if not overwhelming. We, then, zero in on just a few issues. We question those that affect us or those we care about, and we question them when they seem to go against what we otherwise believe or see or experience. When this questioning leads us to realize that what the experts are presenting as true is not so for us, we dig in our heels and prepare for battle. Our children depend upon us. Without us, there is no one else for them.

Chapter 11

Passion

The world is so full of a number of things,
I'm sure we should all be as happy as kings.

- Robert Louis Stevenson

The key to raising children, the key to interaction with everyone, lies in the respect we give them. This is not deference that puts the child above us. It is the acknowledgement of the other's humanness that connects him to us. And it is the recognition of the other's uniqueness that sets him apart from us.

According the child this respect means allowing room for his passion in life to grow. That is the neutral stance – not getting in the way. That is the least we can do. Better is the positive, active stance: doing all we can to help this passion flourish.

There is a natural joy in young children. They are glad to be alive, happy for the day, pleased with what life gives them. What we adults see as simple or mundane thrills them. A little puddle is pure fun. A crawling caterpillar is a wonder to behold – and to hold! A refrigerator box is a week's worth of play.

Their world is filled with wonders to explore. There is no fear. There is only curiosity, love, and trust.

And then . . . what? What happens to this love of life? Where does it go? What squeezes it out? Must it fade into the seriousness of life that most older children and adults adopt? How does one hold onto this passion for life?

It is rarely a single, significant event that suddenly kills this passion for life. More often, it is a series of various actions that, one by one, chip away at the child's zest for life until one day nothing is left.

Take that little puddle. Those are magnets for little children. Water is irresistible. But it cannot be allowed just to stand there. It must be splashed, higher and more loudly each time. That is fun and a great show of power, too. Look at what he can do with his stamping foot.

Of course, young children have no concerns with cleanliness or dryness. Or, at least, they do not have them yet. That is an adult concern. But need it be the child's concern here? Where is the harm in puddle splashing? If clothing gets muddy, it can be washed. Is it really so difficult to throw one more outfit into the washing machine? Or if it is such a concern, dress him in rain clothes – boots, rain pants, rain jacket. And let the merry play continue.

The same is true of many outdoor, childhood delights. Children are kept under guard so often when outside that it would seem their adults believe freedom in such play should never happen. The adults may well have good reasons for these decisions. But the alternative of letting children engage in these pleasures has a minimal effect on adults but tremendous and positive ones on the children. Playing on a dirt mound, rolling down a grassy hill, getting shoes and clothes wet, tangling hair in branches, or, in general, becoming a mess are all inevitable in outdoor play. Is such really so awful? It is just part of being an active child. Children are not so concerned with their appearance. Should they be? They explore their world and learn about it by getting down into it.

But dirt and water and grass stains are just the beginning. The next step is what really bothers adults. Sure, they want their children to look their best. But they also want them perfectly safe. It is one thing to allow mud play in grubby clothes. What about seemingly dangerous play? Where does one draw the line?

When they were little, my children loved to go barefoot in the warmer months. So did their friends. But I was a standout among the parents, for I let mine shake the shoes. That little freedom was great.

Or maybe what really mattered was being in control, being the one to decide whether to strap on sandals or keep the feet free. And the result was . . . ? Their feet were not unscathed. They got their share of nicks and scrapes and cuts. But it must have been worth it, for they still chose to go barefoot when they could.

So does going barefoot ensure the child will retain his passion for life? That it should be so simple! It is merely one little part of a child's existence that lets him enjoy life without adult rules. For it is the many rules and the subsequent reminders and reprimands that wear down a child. Certainly, major, devastating events – loss of a parent or sibling, sexual abuse, life-threatening disease – can erode this joie de vivre. But what most Westernized children encounter day after day are not those life-altering events. Instead, they are showered with rules. "Don't do this. Stay away from that. Keep out of there." It is not just at home. School personnel hand out more of the same: "Keep still. Don't talk. Stay in line." So do employees of stores, officials at parks, even adults at playgrounds: "Don't touch. Keep off. No climbing."

Some rules are necessary for a life among others. Many are not. So many seem arbitrary. So many *are*.

It is half an hour before dinner. Twelve-year-old Ty announces he is going to play at a friend's house down the block. "No," says his dad, "It is too close to dinner." Is it? Ty knows well enough when dinner is, has a watch, is responsible for being home five minutes before dinner. Why should an adult determine whether he can play for that length of time? Why cannot he decide if it is worth getting involved in a game that will have to be terminated in less than 25 minutes? Why cannot he decide how to use his time (as long as it is not hurting anyone or anything)? Ultimately, one must ask, is this an issue in which an adult even needs to be involved? There is no such need.

It is now after dinner and dark. The boys want to play outside. "No, you cannot. It's dark out" comes down the final word from the boy's parents. This is a safe neighborhood. Houses are 20 feet from the street. All have an unobstructed view of cars driving by, sidewalks, and front yards. Street lamps and porch lights are on all along the block. What is wrong with playing in the dark? Does it really matter?

It is pouring outside. My children are waterproofed with rubber boots, rain pants, hooded rain jackets. Off to a neighbor's house they go. "No, he can't play. It's raining out. Too bad your mom makes you go out in the rain instead of staying inside where it's warm and dry." Puddle play and dam building and floating twig races down the street gutter go on without the friend. That was the parent, not the child, speaking; he had not been consulted. The boy loves water play. He would not have minded the rain. Even without rain gear, he plays for hours in the rain when not prevented by his parents. He never seems to get chilled. What good is being served in denying him rain play? Where would have been the harm?

Bit by bit, a child's freedoms are taken away. Senseless rules are made. Arbitrary decisions are handed down.

What hurts most is when these rules run counter to a child's natural inclinations. Young children are meant to run and play outside and move around. They have quiet moments, too. But physically active play is what their bodies demand. Constant reminders to be still and not fidget ignore the child's naturally active spirit. Schools are notorious for working against this aspect of a child's natural need. What, then, is a child to do? It seems prescription drugs are the answer. When we work against what the body demands – physical activity for longer than school recess allows – we are left with few options. Deny nature and turn to drugs, instead.

So we doubly stifle the child's passion for life. First, we fill his world with rules that run counter to his needs. Second, we fill his system with drugs that alter his natural state. How can a child ever hope to lead a passionate life when drugs – prescription or not – control his mind and body?

The current theme for youths is "Just Say No" (to drugs). Drugs, we say, destroy a person. Dependency results. Perceptions and behavior are altered, become unnatural, can become self-destructive. Essentially, one loses control as the drug's effects take over. How is this any different from drugging our children in school? Drugs, illegal or prescription, still alter the person. Supposedly, those using the latter are monitored by a physician. Yet, still, children have unpleasant side effects. With drugs such as Ritalin, too often, the concern is not really for the child. It is for decorum in the classroom. The question asked is "What is wrong with this child?" rather than "What is wrong with this system or environment?" Ultimately, it is easier to drug the child than to change the system. Such a response to the problem of a child being too active or not paying attention in class hardly respects the child.

Allowing the child's passion to grow is more than minimizing the stultifying, arbitrary rules. It means also eliminating from his environment other elements that dull the passion. Foremost among these is television.

Denying one's child access to television is probably the most difficult action a parent can take. I suspect parents would sooner talk about the "birds and the bees" than eliminate television for their child. It is almost seen as a right that no one should deny another.

In fact, American parents, according to Marie Winn in *The Plug-In Drug*, believe it is undemocratic to deny television viewing to their children. It seems not quite fair. Yet many of these same parents do not like the fact that their children watch so much.

Ultimately, the parent, the one who is responsible for looking out for the child's best interests, must ask, is television really in his best interest? Is reluctance to deny him television-viewing grounded in the belief that it is good or at least neutral for him? Or is refusing to limit viewing due to the likely reaction – that there will be tantrums, angry resistance, and, the worst, screams that label the parent as mean, stupid, and hateful?

Yet television viewing is neither good nor even neutral in its impact on viewers. Several excellent books go into depth about this, citing both studies as well as individual instances of the impact television has on the lives of children and families. See especially Winn's *The Plug-In Drug*, Jerry Mander's *Four Arguments for the Elimination of Television*, and Jean Anderson and Robin Wilkins' *Getting Unplugged: Take Control of Your Family's Television, Video Game, and Computer Habits*. The point here is not to repeat what has been already written. Instead, the desire is for us to discover on our own what television does to our children. We can read book after book on the subject, get advice from the experts, and listen to the neighbors. But all of these facts and opinions will have no bearing on our actions until we understand what is happening to our own children. We must see for ourselves.

Remember this book is based on the belief that we, the parents, can assess what is happening to our children. In this case, we are fully capable of discerning the impact of television on our own children. Nothing will be as convincing as one's own experience or observation. To gain such insights, all we need is an openness to see what is truly going on. We need to observe our children during television viewing and soon after they separate from it. What are they doing? How do they look? How do they behave afterwards? What are their interactions with others – family or friends – after leaving television? How does all of this compare to times when they are not or have not been watching television? What kind of language and behavior are they picking up from it?

If we are really brave, we will also listen to our gut feeling. We may not have at hand specific examples to support what we feel, but our intuition brings in unnamed instances – ones that lie just below the surface of consciousness – that we did not think important enough to pay attention to. Our intuition is like a summary chapter. It takes into account all the little bits and pieces over an extended period of time and puts them together to make a sensible explanation. It can be hard to listen to our gut feeling because we often do not have the hard evidence to support what we feel. But when we learn to listen – and to filter out interferences such as our own fear or guilt – we will come up with the right answer. But the right answer is often not the one we want to hear.

We need to be honest with ourselves. Are we using the television to keep the children quiet? Are we using a babysitter whose language and encouragement to BUY BUY BUY we allow in our home only because the price is right? Would we allow a hired babysitter to behave so to our children – to use foul language, to speak disrespectfully to others, to tell the children always to want more? Are we avoiding this issue of television watching because we dread having to take appropriate action? Do we so fear our children's resistance that we choose to do nothing?

Respecting the child does not equate to giving him what he asks for. We satisfy his *needs*, not necessarily his *wants*. We guide him to help him become all that he can be. Living his passion is part of realizing this potential. Is that achieved by his spacing out in front of the television? Do we honor what is best in our child by permitting such to take place? These are not hard questions. But the answers may be difficult to give honestly.

Each of us answers in her own way. Seventeen years ago, I was prompted to ask myself these very questions. My oldest two were preschoolers at the time. I found that I was letting the children watch more and more as time went on. It was so easy. I knew where they were, I saw they were quiet, and I had large chunks of time for myself. At night, it calmed them before bedtime. Did I mention these were "good" shows – *Sesame Street* and PBS nature programs?

But I did not like that I was using the television as a babysitter. And the time they were spending was truly a waste. Absolutely nothing of value was being learned that could not be learned better and more quickly in some other way. They were spending time with a thing at the expense of time with a human being.

So I shut it off. Television was off-limits for all of us, all of the time. (Well, my husband still watched. It was only occasionally and in a room apart from the rest of us. Yet even he eventually came around. Now the television is used only for periodic video movie rentals.) Doing this when the children were young made it far easier than putting it off until they were older. There was little resistance, the habit was not well ingrained, and they were (are) generally cooperative children. This is not to say that it was smooth sailing from the start. While viewing television at home was eliminated, the desire to watch was not. There remained the temptation to watch television at friends' homes. And that temptation was sometimes indulged in. But that was rare, and, for the most part, the children lived quite well without television.

Eliminating television freed up significant time for us. We now, for instance, had more time for bedtime stories. Recently, I came across an advertisement in a magazine that listed about six "ingredients" that parents use to "grow" an infant into an adult over the course of 18 years. Among them was "five bedtime stories" read to the child over these 18 years. Possibly, had I kept television as the quieting influence for bedtime, my children would have had a similarly miniscule number of bedtime stories under their belts. As it is, that number is ludicrous. The number is closer to two thousand. As I write this, I am in the midst of reading the unabridged version (with more than 1,400 pages) of *The Count of Monte Cristo* by Alexandre Dumas to my 13-year-old. With television, we never would have even attempted it.

But eliminating television did not necessarily mean time with Mom took up the slack. Certainly, I filled in some of the gaps as with reading bedtime stories. Most of the freed-up time, instead, went to individual play. The result was and continues to be a high degree of creativity in all three children. When one has large blocks of time to fill, inventiveness comes to the rescue. And because it is the individual who has come up with the method to occupy himself, he will identify with it. It is his. Whether it is blocks built into a tower (which he, of course, knocks down), a puppet show with handmade puppets and scenery, a paper towel holder made for Mom's birthday, or any of a gazillion other projects, the one chosen is his alone. This is where the passion enters: while one is occupied with a self-devised project. No one has ever before done it just that way; it is his own and special endeavor. He has reason to be involved, intent, and excited.

Television shows can be enjoyable, but they are not exciting. They lack the direct involvement. They are a passive entertainment. Worse, they are mesmerizing to the point that many find it difficult to stop watching. My oldest child, Rhiannon, still remembers watching television and being in a sort of trance. She was facing the screen, but she was looking beyond it, through it, in a sense.

Not all children react in the same way. Just as there are some children who do not much care for sugary treats (yes, I have met some; they do exist), so there are some who have little desire for television. My second-born, Rikki, is one. She could not abide being plunked in front of the boob tube for more than 45 minutes. She had to be doing something, instead. There was no danger of her being mesmerized. Nor would television ever drain her of her passion for life. (When she did go to a friend's house to watch television, it was a one-time only occurrence and was done more for curiosity and for wanting to be with her friend than for television viewing by itself.) But that reaction seems to be the exception. Most children will not willingly remove themselves from viewing nor eliminate it wholly from their lives. This is where we parents who know our children and have their best interests in mind come in. We remember the big picture. It is not the full-size television screen, but what they are becoming. So we help them keep their passions alive. We provide the environments where these passions can flourish.

It is not only the environment that contributes to or detracts from developing our children's passions. It is also sometimes our actions that affect them. We place them in a school that leaves little room for self-expression, that treats all as alike in ability, interests, and styles of learning, that provides no time for pursuing passions in depth. And then we force them to stay when we see the results are not good. Yet options are always available if only we remain open to see them. There are other teachers, other schools, other ways of learning, including correspondence schools, homeschooling, and tutoring. When we say we can do nothing else, indeed we cannot. But the moment we open ourselves to the possibility of other options, that is when we are finally able to see what can be done.

Openness is so important. We need it when observing our children in order to understand what is really taking place. But this receptivity to other ideas does more than help us to see what *is*. It also allows us to see what *can be*. Through an open mind, we see the possibilities, the options open to us, the paths we may take.

Remaining open to the possibilities enters all aspects of our life. The more often we practice openness, the more likely it is to become a habit. It is self-reinforcing because the results of openness are so rewarding. The world opens before us where before it was closed off.

The advantage of being open to all possibilities was driven home several years ago when Keith and I were on our way to a hike in the mountains. A streambed that was supposedly fordable by car was before us. We cautiously drove through it and just as cautiously got stuck. We were in the middle of the creek, in the middle of nowhere, during the middle of the week. No one was around and there were no nearby homes.

When Keith saw we were stuck, he began his calculations. In order to get help, someone would have to walk the four miles back to the main road, hitch a ride into town, find a gas station, hire a tow truck, drive back, and finally pull out our car.

With Keith's method, the day would be shot. We would have no hike. It would be utter frustration, a loss of money as well as time. That seemed a poor solution to me. I was determined to get our hike in and not sacrifice the day to a car extraction. That meant we would drive the car forward. (The trailhead was still some distance away.) It also meant that we would drive through it a second time on our return. I knew there had to be a way for us to get our car through the streambed ourselves.

There was.

We used the tire jack to raise the car. Once raised, that section's tire had rocks and large boards (conveniently left in the stream) placed beneath it. Then we switched to a tire on the opposite side of the car and repeated the procedure. Bit by bit, we made progress, switching from one tire to another. It took awhile. The water was cold. And the stream obviously had runoff from the nearby cow pastures. But we accomplished our task in plenty of time to allow us to do our hike. And on the way back, we were not nearly so cautious in crossing; going faster kept us from getting stuck.

Why was there the difference in solutions considered? Why had Keith not even thought of jacking up the car? Why had going for help been his only option? It was the mindset. Keith believed there was no way for our car to drive through the stream, especially as we had spun the wheels and put the vehicle deeper and deeper into the bed. Believing there was no way to drive the car through prevented him from finding or devising a solution along such a line. His mind was set; there was only one possibility. Only outside help could rescue us. I, on the other hand, was completely open to finding a solution that involved only us.

Possibilities exist. What is, is not only what can be. More is available as long as we allow ourselves to realize it. We do not need to limit ourselves or our children. We do not have to accept the joy being pounded out of our children in school. Some parents accept such developments as natural, as part of the child adjusting to the "real world." Others do not accept. They switch schools or teachers. They homeschool for a year or more. They realize that passion for life is important and no school or teacher is so good that their child's passion for life should be sacrificed.

I have seen both sides. Regrettably, keeping the child in a certain school, despite the child losing his zest for life, happens all too often. It is not just that school no longer holds an interest. It is that that feeling also carries over into the rest of the child's life. Where before the child was thrilled to play after school, now only television holds an attraction. Even friends cannot draw him away.

On the other side, children whose parents see the changes taking place and work to correct them see positive effects. As mentioned earlier, there is at the least the realization by the child that the parent recognizes the problem and is doing something about it. The parent is working with the child to help him. Through this understanding, the parent is able to find an educational environment better suited to the child. It is a learning process for both parent and child. And the result is a child still learning but much happier.

My second child, Rikki, was one who, over the course of her year in first grade, gradually lost this zest for learning. Even her teacher remarked on this change. It was a supposedly good school and a good and caring teacher. But the methods were not right for Rikki. A change in the following fall saw a return to her old self. But even then, the full effects of that one year were not entirely corrected for several more years.

Sometimes, it is our less obvious actions that contribute to eroding the child's love of life. How we conduct our own lives has a bearing on what our children do. The example we set will always speak more forcefully than our spoken words.

What kind of example are we providing to our children? They are learning, growing, aiming for adulthood. Are we showing them good reasons for wanting to be adults? Do we ourselves have a passion for life? Does learning still excite us? Does a new day still hold wonders to explore? Or are we, instead, comfortably settled into a routine, boring existence?

I call those in the latter category the "walking dead." For them, one day is as much the same as another. Each is as boring as the next. They go to work, come home, eat, collapse on the couch in front of the television, then go to bed. The next day it all begins once more. Is this a life we want our children to aim for? Is this all there is until that far-off retirement?

It is not that jobs are boring. It is not that work is exhausting. It is not that one day is much like the other.

Those situations may or may not be true. But what matters most is how we approach our jobs or life itself. Do we allow it to be boring? Do we allow the sameness to overwhelm while ignoring the variety in a day? Do we wait for excitement to come our way while doing nothing ourselves to create excitement?

Or do we, instead, emerge from our deadness? Do we make our lives a joy? If Viktor Frankl, as related in *A Man's Search for Meaning*, could love life even while in the Nazi concentration camps, surely we can maintain our passion for life in our comfortable surroundings.

Such a passionate attitude toward life is infectious. We affect others by it in two ways. First, we set the example, the expectation, even, of the individual making the most of her life. We show that it can be done. We show how it can be done. And we demonstrate its effects.

Second, those effects rub off onto those around us. A depressed person has a sobering effect on all who come near him. Likewise, one thrilled with life enthuses others or at least brightens a few moments of the day for them. In either case, having such a passionate approach to life has a positive effect on our children.

This is not to say we strive for all walking around with fake smiles on our faces. The aim is not smiles, but a true appreciation for life, which inevitably brings smiles.

A significant contributor to having this zest for life is how much control we feel we have in our lives. If we feel powerless, we are not likely to care much at all about life.

Yet Frankl retained his passion for life even in the depressing conditions of a concentration camp. How is that possible? In any situation we always have at least one of two options. If conditions are not to our liking, we can either change those conditions or change our attitude toward them. This means we always have control over our own lives, even in the worst of circumstances.

In *Flow: The Psychology of Optimal Experience*, Mihaly Csikszentmihalyi cites several examples of prisoners in solitary confinement who realized this. These were people who chose life. They did not allow their circumstances to overwhelm them. For these men and women, there was only one option. They could not escape physically, so they escaped mentally. They changed their attitude toward their situation. They occupied their minds with games such as chess, with creative activities such as poetry composition, or with imaginary travel, including detailed descriptions of what was seen and done on the way.

The power of the mind in such circumstances is especially illustrated with the story of the United States Air Force pilot who was in solitary confinement in a jungle in Vietnam for many years. Although he lost 80 pounds and was not in the best of health, upon his release, he played, at his insistence, a game of golf. Much to everyone's astonishment, he played a superb game. The secret was in his mental preparation. During his imprisonment he had played golf over and over in his mind. Which clubs to use, how to approach the ball, how to play any particular course (because he did not play the same mental golf course each time) were all practiced during the seemingly infinite stretches of time. His body, then, was merely an extension of his mind. After so much practice he, of course, played an excellent game.

Is this passion for life? Indeed it is. One cannot survive such extremes without having a powerful drive to live. This is not desperation, a last ditch effort to be free. No, that hopelessness was what, in Alexander Solzhenitsyn's account of Soviet prisons, drove some prisoners to hurl themselves into the barbed wire. That was, in essence, suicide; that was the complete opposite of a passionate desire for life. Passion for life, through such mental "games," retains life.

Children use the same mental techniques in less desperate circumstances. Richard Louv, in *Childhood's Future*, describes how he crisscrossed the country talking to children about, among several topics, daycare. With few exceptions, those still in daycare, when asked about their experience with it, said it was fine. Those who had been but no longer were still in daycare talked, instead, about how much they had disliked it. The older the child was, the more negative was his evaluation of his daycare experience. Why the discrepancy? Had conditions changed so drastically in just a few years and all over the United States to make what was once an unpleasant experience now acceptable?

The author remained perplexed, but he need not have been. Children in daycare have no choice. They can not opt out. And they know well enough that it would be futile to ask their parents to remove them from daycare. The circumstances are set. How, then, can they make their situation bearable? They do not like it, but they cannot escape. Their only option is to alter their perception of their circumstances. By convincing themselves that the situation is "fine," it is then acceptable to them. They can live with it.

That is, until circumstances change. Once they no longer must be in daycare, their attitude need no longer make up for what they see as unacceptable circumstances. A mental cover-up is no longer needed. They can be honest about what it was like.

Again, our goal is not fake smiles or forced enthusiasm. But there will be times when we or our children are in situations similar to those of children in daycare; we cannot alter the circumstance and must in some way cope. Then, such mental games we can play. We make the best of the situation, controlling our attitude if nothing else.

Yet the ideal that we parents aim to provide for ourselves as well as for our children is an environment where that zest for life springs naturally from us.

Children under normal circumstances are naturally enthused with life. We support this when we minimize the arbitrary rules, provide an outlet for their natural propensity for active and outdoor play, and set a good example with our own passionate embrace of life.

This passion for life is intimately tied to our beliefs about work. It both affects our work and is affected by it. When we work without a passionate interest, we are merely putting in time on the job. It is only a job and likely one where the income is all that matters. It is a routine, a dead-end, something which we must do to live (and possibly support others in the family.)

Such an attitude is not dependent upon the job. Even the seemingly most routine jobs can be approached with passion. And those we would call exciting can be boring to workers who just do not care. Take any job. Look at those working and compare the attitudes. Those who are in it only for the money or who just hate being there are in stark contrast to those who have a desire to be there and find pleasure in every moment.

Consider, for instance, dental offices. Over the years I have seen my share of them. In one, a children's dental office, no less, everyone was so serious that a black cloud hung permanently over all the rooms. A smile never escaped the receptionist's lips, a kind word was never heard, a pleasant time was never experienced. In another, also a dental practice specializing in children, everyone was happy. Where the other office was dominated by melancholy (or doom, patients there might say), this one had sunshine and joy. The receptionist joked with the parents. Children were recognized and spoken to with consideration as well as levity. All left with good feelings.

The jobs of both receptionists were the same: schedule the patients, note their arrival and departure, relay information to and from the dentist. Yet a world separated the two in execution of the given tasks. The first had no love of her work. The second's love for what she did overflowed and touched everyone with whom she came in contact. And then this love all came back to her.

When the first receptionist goes home, what does she take with her? She has relief that the job is over, negative feelings about how her time was spent, stories about patients who were difficult. What does the second receptionist take with her? She takes home pleasure from a job well-done, jokes shared, stories of silly children.

We have examples all around us of people who likewise exude their joy for life. We know that the enthusiastic happiness for life need not end in childhood. It need not be stifled by education. It need not be buried by a job.

So how does one hold on to this passion? Better, how does one ensure that our children keep it? For, although we all want our children to demonstrate self-sufficiency by supporting themselves when adults, we want more. We want them to be like that second dental receptionist and love their jobs.

As with all presented in this book, the key lies in observing children. While there are many children who run at the mere mention of chores, those who enjoy work are not so few in number.

But first we must examine what is meant by work. A job is work. Or is it? If one's job is to exercise horses but one loves riding, is that work? Or is it pleasure? If one is a counselor but one enjoys talking with people, is the job work or fun? If one is an accountant but enjoys working with numbers, is the job work or enjoyment?

At home, some hire people to do their garden and yard work. For others, this same work is relaxation, fresh air, and exercise; they could not be paid to stop.

Look at little children. By some definitions, what they do all day is work. Most adults would consider learning a foreign language "work." Yet infants spend much of their time learning to speak what is an unknown tongue to them. Is this work? For those who through injury or surgery have temporarily lost the use of a leg, learning to walk is work. For infants who have never before walked, is the same work to them?

In all cases, it is effort being expended. But whether that effort is called work or considered play is really in the mind of the individual. One person's work is another's play. Or, put another way, what one calls work need not be so.

Our family lives in the city where houses are closely spaced and front yard fences are few. We know our neighbors and are aware of their comings and goings. When one has a project going on, everyone knows about it. When our children were young and they saw a neighbor embarking on yet another project, they would rush over. They wanted to help. No, dollar signs were not in their eyes. They enjoyed the work for the sake of it. They never asked for pay and often were not offered it.

There was one memorable time that a neighbor had had a truckload of bark delivered. He hired two youths from a few blocks away to haul it via wheelbarrow to the back yard. Ty, who was seven and a half at the time, asked if he could help. He had no thoughts of earning money. He only wanted to join in the fun. Fortunately, he was allowed to help. Although years younger than the other two boys, Ty worked both more consistently and longer. He was, after all, "working" for the pleasure of it and not for money.

That last word is what I have found to be the all-important piece in this work-play conundrum. I have never paid my children to do work around the house. Nor did I call their efforts "work." Instead they were helping me. Or, to better understand their perspective, they were joining me in my adult work. As their goal was to become an adult, being able to perform adult work was a privilege to them. They felt adult-like in doing what I was doing – and doing it well enough to be allowed to continue.

This idea is addressed by Ruth Benedict ("Continuities and Discontinuities in Cultural Conditioning," *Psychiatry* I, 1938: 161-167). She describes how an elder asks a very little girl to close the door. It is a very heavy door and no easy task for her. Everyone patiently waits as she struggles to close it. No one rushes to help her. Nor does anyone pay her to do it. The job is deemed within her capability and thus given to her. On her part, she wishes to demonstrate that she is able to perform, that she is now older, stronger, more capable. That is, she is progressing on her path to adulthood.

When money is injected into children's work-play, interesting things happen. What was fun or pleasurable no longer is. More, by being paid for work, the intrinsic value is overwhelmed by the extrinsic rewards.

We saw this demonstrated with reading. For some children, reading is a chore. Some are just learning to read, some older ones never quite understand the written letters-spoken sound connection, and some know how to read but just do not enjoy it. Some young friends fell into the latter category. One was paid 50 cents for each book she read. Another was paid several dollars. Then there was my oldest who was a few years younger than these two friends. She was never paid to read. Who read the most? It was the one with no reward, my daughter Rhiannon. Who read the least despite rewards and urgings? Of course, it was the one who had the highest monetary incentive.

Rewards, monetary or otherwise, say that this task is so onerous that one would do it only if compensated. There is no other benefit, no internal reward, so an external one must be given. In the above example, reading was a burden for some. The monetary incentive only emphasized that aspect to the child. Instead of compensating the child for his perceived unpleasantness of reading, the money reinforced that idea. Really, if reading is so wonderful, why should the child be paid to do it?

We have another friend who is just learning to read. Because her progress is slower than many, she is rewarded with toys after each reading session. She has told us she, indeed, wants to have these reading sessions. But it is not because she enjoys reading. It is not because she wants to be able to read. It is not because she wants to discover the worlds that books and all that is in print has to offer. It is simply because she wants to get the toys. So what happens when the toys stop? Or rather, why will she continue to read when her only reason for doing so is removed?

Will children work if they are not compensated by us? I have certainly found this so. Most parents have also. They have experienced their little ones imitating their actions and trying, even if not offered the opportunity, to help with adult work.

But this wonderful state of affairs does not last forever. From about four to six years of age, my daughter Rikki loved to sweep. She practically begged me to let her sweep our floors. I was all too happy to comply, especially since she did such a thorough job. But that state lasted only about two years. What happened?

During this period in her life, Rikki was mastering this skill. Young children naturally do this. They repeat an action over and over again. Watch a toddler who has just discovered how to pour water. He would rival the Sorcerer's Apprentice in water used if allowed to. He cannot pour enough – from faucet to pitcher to glass to sink (or for water conserving families, back to pitcher). Mastery of a skill, however mundane to us, comes only with practice.

Once mastered, the work will continue for some time. If it is seen as adult work, the child will still do it to show that he has acquired this adult skill. Engaging in adult activities – and doing them as well as adults – demonstrates that the child is on his way to adulthood. That is, after all, the child's goal – to become an adult.

I remember well when I was a child and our family acquired a new riding lawnmower. It was one that I, at 14, and my 12-year-old brother were allowed to use. "Allowed" is the correct word. It was a privilege for us, a mark of our capabilities, a sign that we were becoming adults. Previously, only my father was able to handle the old, heavier mower. Now my brother and I joined his ranks.

Not surprisingly, this privilege soon turned into a chore. Was it because we were paid? It does seem strange to be paid for doing what we considered a special honor. So the compensation may have played a part in our lessening enthusiasm for mowing. Too, it consumed several hours of our precious free time each week. We may have resented that loss, especially during the school year. And the novelty could last only so long. That is, we soon mastered this adult skill, so we were ready to move on and try our hands at some other adult job.

But we could not. We had no choice in the matter. Each of us mowed a certain section of our five-acre yard. And it had to be done each week.

In contrast, I look at my 13-year-old son who has been taking care of a neighbor's yard for at least three years. He has total control in the work. He decides when to mow depending upon the weather, how long the grass is, and what his plans are for the rest of the day. He decides what to do – whether mowing alone is sufficient, whether edging is needed, whether weeding of the garden is called for. All of this takes many hours each week. He sees that his work is at least as good as that of the lawn care services and is better than the work of many adults in the area. So he takes great pride in his work.

Ty's work is necessary, important, adult work. So was my lawn mowing. But the fact that he is in control, as are most adults who care for their own lawns, puts him more in an adult role than my brother and I were. Because it is known that Ty is the one who does the work, he is sought after. Other neighbors see his work and want him to care for their yards as well. So his pride is based on his own perception of the quality of his work, knowing that it measures up to adult work, and on what others say.

On the surface, this comparison to adult work seems to contradict what was previously said about children wanting no evaluations. It was claimed before that children want neither criticism nor praise, but only acceptance. They may ask for advice on a project, but unsolicited comments are generally not appreciated. Yet here is a boy glad to have his labors judged on an adult scale.

For Ty, acceptance is primarily what he wants. Acceptance of his work takes the form of payment by his customers and demand for more work by other potential clients. Obviously, some evaluation does occur in that the neighbors see his work and compare it to work they would do. But this is not the same as the comments, good or bad, that children prefer not to hear. He does not have an adult watching over his every move. He does not have someone constantly checking his progress. Once he has a job, he does not get evaluations. What comments he does receive are gratitude for doing the job and directions for other work to be done.

Every family has chores that must be done for the household to operate effectively. It is only natural that each member contribute according to his or her capabilities. But interests also play a role. Cooking is usually done by the parent who enjoys it – or dislikes it the least. It is the same with car maintenance, yard work, cleaning, and other jobs around the house. If parents can choose which chores they will do, why not allow the children to do so also? As long as certain parameters are met, children can be allowed some control in their work done around the house. For instance, a certain amount of time must be put in by each child, certain jobs must be done on a regular basis, and selection of jobs must be made at least a week in advance.

The more control the child has, the better. This assumes that respect for the child is maintained. However much a five-year-old may want to mow the lawn, it is not likely to be safe enough for him. On the other hand, if a three-year-old wishes to wash dishes, there is little harm in letting him. When a child takes on a difficult task (difficult but not dangerous), there is a good reason to let him. The job may take much, much longer to finish. But any child working at a self-chosen job, especially one that is seen as an adult's, will want to finish. And he will likely do a very fine job.

When Ty was four years old, he relieved his dad of his dishwashing duty one evening. Every item took minutes to wash and rinse. The whole job took more than an hour. This was, after all, a family of five. Yet he never rushed. Care was extended until the end.

Having some control in the selection of jobs helps. Having control over when the jobs are done helps, also. This, of course, varies by job. The garbage can must be out by a certain time, but still the child can decide whether to do it the morning of garbage collection, the night before, or the afternoon before. Knowing what are the natural consequences of not doing the job on time helps as well. "Natural" consequences mean just that as opposed to, say, a nagging or angry parent. So with the garbage, if not put out in time, the child may have to pay for extra pick-up the following week. With, say, lawn mowing, a delay may result in the job taking considerably longer because the grass has grown so thick and tall. Or, because the lawn looks unacceptably unsightly, someone else may have to do the work and be appropriately compensated by the child. (Such consequences should be explained in advance.) Ultimately, if the job is consistently not done, the responsibility for that job may need to be removed.

What we try to avoid is the practice of slave labor. When we respect another, whether child or adult, we do not order the person about. So we would not, for instance, make our child get a can of soda for us from the kitchen because we are too lazy to get up ourselves. Would we order a friend to do that? Here the idea extends to regular and more extensive work. The idea is not necessarily to give the child those jobs that are least pleasant. That would be abusing the power of the parent. Instead, our responsibility is to take into consideration for the child those factors that we do for ourselves. So just as we share the pleasant tasks, so, too, do we share the less desirable ones. And just as we would not take on a job beyond our capabilities, so, too, would we not impose such upon the child. We adults do make mistakes, as many a plumber will testify. So we have no cause to be harsh should the child take on a job which he then learns is too much for him. There is always room for correcting mistakes, always flexibility in job assignments, always recognition that accidents happen.

In the end, every household has unpleasant tasks that must be done. And it is likely that each member will have a share in them. Whether one is paid or not, whether one gets to choose the specific job, whether one has any control over how or when the job is done, all pale behind the child's attitude about the job. How does he approach it? Does he fight it, argue about doing it, or try to delay it in the hopes of avoiding it altogether? Does he do it with resentment, see the job as an unfair burden, hate every second of the chore? Is he like the receptionist mentioned previously who carries a black cloud over her the whole time she is on the job? Or is he like the second receptionist who seems to love the job and spreads that positive feeling to all who come in contact with her?

In any endeavor, the choice of attitude is the child's. We can set up the best environment, but the child's reaction is his own. Where we can help is with the attitude we adopt in similar circumstances. Our example here matters as much as it does in any other aspect of the child's life. Any job can be made enjoyable. All it takes is a positive attitude. This we can show as we go about our own work. We can sing, laugh, hum, or just smile as we work.

Conversation and a friendly companion make any drudgery seem less so. Children know this as well as adults do. When my children were young, they often set up lemonade and cookie stands on hot days. Their take for the day depended upon several factors, including the number of people selling. The more people helping, the less money each one received since the total was divided evenly among them. Even though it meant they made less money individually, they always preferred to have friends sit with them and help out. It made the time go by faster and more pleasantly. The reduced income was well worth it.

Work companions for our children need not be peers. We, too, can join forces with them as they work with us. If the child has not discovered how to make light of a task, we can show him as we work beside him. This is not doing the job for the child, but doing it *with* him. For instance, one can scrub the toilet while the other cleans the sink. Not too long ago, many a sibling grew up washing dishes while another dried them. Partners make any job more pleasant. And when the children are older and free time with family members becomes a rare commodity, working side by side is a wonderful opportunity for time together.

Just as it is various, seemingly insignificant circumstances that can bit by bit erode a child's passion for life, so, too, it is the little things that can add to it. So we minimize the confining rules but also provide plenty of freedom for the child's exuberance to flourish. We eliminate passion-squashing elements such as television but also provide opportunities for engaging in passionate interests. We refuse to treat the children as slaves for work but allow and encourage help with adult work. And always, we set the good example of living a passionate life ourselves.

Chapter 12

Being There

Here I am,
Little Jumping Joan;
When nobody's with me,
I'm all alone.

We parents need to set a good example. Implied in this is that the parent is present. The child must see the parent in action. Or at least, parent and child must be together so a discussion can even ensue.

For the child, there is no substitute for the parent being there. This is true for all ages. "Being there" does not necessarily mean hovering or being intensely involved. Nor does it mean the same degree of involvement at all stages of the child's life. The physically close and constant attachment of the early months is an extreme that is not normally repeated for the child. From there on, the child moves toward independence. It is rarely a smooth path, more often one that seems to have back turns or sidesteps as much as forward movement. The child is constantly testing: is he ready for more freedom and will the adults let him have it? During such explorations, the child still wants the adult around. She is his security, his source of stability in the storm. It is she to whom he returns when trials are too much. It is still she to whom he looks for guidance.

We live in a world that says although children might need parents, others can fill that need, too. In fact, popular with the media and many politicians has been the idea that children need not only parents but a whole village to be properly brought into adulthood. This is well and good, except for the fact that the great majority of us do not live in villages.

In villages, everyone knows everyone else. Many are close relatives. These villages are held together by a common culture that dictates how life is to be lived, what belief system is practiced, what roles are appropriate for different members. It can be a limiting experience in that what has been done for generations is what is still done. But for the same reasons, it holds great security. Everyone knows his or her role, how to relate to others, what is expected in specific situations.

Most of us do not have such villages in which to raise our children. Instead, we have humongous, impersonal cities. Neighbors often do not know each other and rarely talk to one another. And what is the point, given how frequently families move from home to home? Most "inhabitants" are not even around during the day. If not at work, the adults are shopping or travelling here and there. The elderly, a culture's wise ones, are often away from the rest of the community and herded together in "assisted-living" communities or senior citizen centers. Likewise, children, those who most benefit from being around people of all ages, are corralled together with their same-age peers.

Those few who are home can hardly be said to be part of a common culture with others in their area. Politics, religion, social expectations, and more all vary from one individual to another. Even how to raise children cannot be agreed upon.

When we hear that it takes a village to raise a child, we imagine many trusted and familiar individuals having a positive influence on the young members of our society. But that phrase is really intended to have us believe that daycare, schools, camps, sports, etc., are good because they are all part of the child's village. It is meant to make us feel comfortable in letting strangers watch over our children. It is an attempt to assuage feelings of guilt for abandoning our children to people we hardly know.

We fool only ourselves and shortchange our children when we claim our impersonal cities are like villages for raising our young. They are not.

This is not to say that other adults cannot – or should not - watch over our children. Certainly, there are many qualified adults who can care for our children, educate them, guard them from harm. Children themselves can do this. They can care for themselves, fix their own meals, be responsible for getting to and from home and school.

But the question is not, *can* children care for themselves? Nor is it, *can* other adults care for them? The question is, what is in the child's best interest?

Children want their parents. Children say this in various ways. Sometimes, they say so directly to the parents although the parents do not always hear the words. So it was one time with Ty and his dad. "Concentration" was a favorite card game for my children to play, especially with their dad. Once when he was four years old, Ty told his dad he wanted to play the game with him. As Keith was busy washing dishes, he suggested Ty play with his older sister. No, Ty had no desire to play with her. Keith found this incomprehensible. Daughter Rhiannon could play Concentration as well as he could. Why would Ty not play with her instead? The error in his interpretation was believing that the focus was on the game, implying that any competent opponent would satisfy Ty's need. That was not the case. It was the player that mattered most. The game itself was not important. Concentration was merely the means for engaging his father.

Sometimes, the children say pointedly that they want their parents. But instead of speaking to the parents, those who can do something about the situation, they tell other adults. So Richard Louv, the previously mentioned author of *Childhood's Future*, got an earful from the children he spoke with. In fact, the title of the first chapter in his book says it all: "I'll Play with You Tomorrow." The children, like Ty, want time with their parents. But that time is always put off. As one boy tells Louv, "My dad works morning till night, and my mom works afternoons and nights, so they say, 'Tomorrow we're gonna do some things,' but tomorrow comes and they go to work." Sometimes, it is not work, directly, that interferes with giving time to the children. It is the exhaustion from work. So another boy describes how his dad says the same thing, that he'll play with his son tomorrow, but when tomorrow comes, the man just watches television.

Time with Mom or Dad is what the child wants. Even a sibling is an inadequate substitute. Imagine, then, how daycare workers, teachers, and other adults measure up as substitutes by the children. They fall far short. Imagine, too, how children feel when their parents choose time with someone or some*thing*, rather than their children. When the parent spends his precious free time watching television, what is a child to think?

A parent might well reply that watching television with his child *is* spending time with him. They *are* doing something together. Well, yes and no. Unfortunately, such thinking is far too common. A study of time parents spent with their children provided insightful differences of perception. In *Ask the Children: What America's Children Really Think about Working Parents* by Ellen Galinsky, parents and children were questioned about instances that they spent together. Frequently, times a parent, often the father, said he spent with his child was not one the child saw as time together. For instance, the father would be reading the newspaper in the den while his daughter set the table in the dining room. He saw that as time together. She, who experienced no interactions nor even exchanged words, did not see it as time together. Too often, parents claimed time together when it was merely occupying the same building.

"Being present" means more than mere occupancy of the same physical space. Even being in the same room watching television together hardly qualifies. Watching television does not allow for discussions, for explorations of problems the child is having, for opportunities to learn from the parent's example. At most, it allows for laughter at the same joke or viewing of the same home run. Watching television is not doing. But children want to do with their parents.

Even my daughter Rikki has commented on how parents who are with their children are not truly present for them. She sees instances of this all of the time at the zoo, a favorite haunt in her study of animals – and of people interactions, as well. Regardless of the weather, it is almost always crowded. People of all ages love to visit, but families especially enjoy the zoo. It provides a wonderful opportunity for parents to interact with their children. Yet what Rikki sees are many children trying to make that connection, trying to engage their parents, trying to share their excitement but failing miserably. Yes, the parents are physically there with their children. But their attention is elsewhere, more often than not going to an oh-so-important conversation on their cell phone.

Children need time with parents. If denied it, they will let us know about it one way or another. If children do not tell us directly, they will tell us indirectly. My son, Ty, said this by kicking our dog when he could not get the attention he needed from his father. Another young child acted similarly when it was the family dog that went to work with his mom while he went to daycare. Another child tells his mom he wants her around rather than the in-home sitter.

Other children say nothing because they know it will make no difference. The parents believe they must work, so care by others is the only option. This was shown in those children who complained about daycare only after they no longer had to be in such a situation.

Is this a surprise that our children want time with us? Does this not make sense? Would we not expect children to want to be with their parents? And more, when we make the conscious decision to bring children into the world, is it not natural, even expected, to want to spend time with them?

We want our values and beliefs and traditions carried on by our children. How can we expect this to happen when a significant number of hours of the child's waking day is spent with another?

On their part, children look to their parents. When very young, however much they may disobey or refuse to cooperate or assert their independence, they still look to their parents as gods. These adults who figure so large in their lives know everything, can do anything. The children want to be like them. They will work beside the parent, not only learning how to perform the task but also trying to *be* like this much-revered parent. It is not just mastering adult work that the young child is after. Certainly, such is part of growing up. But the child wants more than the ability to perform as an adult. He also wants to be just like Daddy.

This halcyon period does not last forever. The child eventually moves beyond wanting to be just like Daddy to incorporating his own individuality into the picture. But this still includes the parent. There is still reverence and respect, at least for certain aspects of the parent. An older child's rebellion does not mean total rejection of the parents and all they represent. It is merely an attempt to find his place in the world, to define himself as someone beyond his father and mother's son. By becoming the unique individual that he is meant to be, the child incorporates bits and pieces of those he admires and respects. The ones who figure prominently in this picture are the parents.

And how can a child do this when the parent is not around? What is to be learned from an absent parent? How can a child even know his parents' values when time together is minimal?

Values, morals, ways of looking at the world cannot be learned merely by getting a list. One learns by encountering different situations, good and bad, and dealing with them. But it is the guidance of a person more experienced, wiser, and more knowledgeable who ensures the child's reaction to the situation will be proper, if not this time, then at least eventually. Discussions take place. Stories of similar experiences by the parent occur. Suggestions of what to do next time are given. This all takes time. And it takes timing. One must be there to discuss. But one must be around when the need arises. Waiting until the working parent has time on the weekend may be too late.

The idea of quality time does not satisfy. Does it make sense that a child will save up all that needs to be discussed for those two hours set aside on Saturday? After any absence, a time of reacquainting is needed. A base of mutuality must be reestablished. Only then can one open up and talk about what matters. Especially for the older child, significant time is needed just for him to feel comfortable bringing up a topic of concern. These are not issues that can be packed up and drawn out at a moment's notice.

A friend illustrated this point recently. She is a single parent, and she alone was responsible for raising her daughter. Her job kept her away from home for the usual hours during the workweek, that is, until dinnertime. Once home, she would have this typical conversation.

Mom: "How was school?"
Daughter: "Fine."
Mom: "What did you do?"
Daughter: "Oh, just the usual."

Mom: "How's your friend Lori doing?"
Daughter: "She's good."

Then one year, this woman took a sabbatical from work. This allowed her to be present when her daughter returned home from school. The same questions were asked, but there were no longer typical answers. Instead of getting dead-end responses, this mother received book-length replies. The only difference between before and now was the timing. She was available when the need to talk was strongest with her daughter. Two hours later, it was gone. Before, the daughter may have vented to school friends about these cares and concerns and events of the day. Or she may have just buried it inside herself.

Regardless, the extent of the responses indicated how much the girl did have to say, how important it was to talk, how great was the need. On her part, the mother also realized how much she had missed in all those previous years – hundreds and hundreds of days – when she had not been there. That could never be retrieved. She realized, too, what her daughter had missed by not having her mother around when needed. There had been no readily available sounding board, no mother's words of comfort, no all-caring presence that makes a home a sought-after refuge from the outside onslaughts of the world.

During a brief period in her life, another friend maintained a weekend marriage. For several months, she worked in a city hundreds of miles distant from her husband. When they got together on the weekend, much of the time was devoted to just reestablishing their relationship. There was hardly time for new issues to be dealt with. Should we expect anything different from children? It is not easy to bring up problems at the mere request of the parent. "What's bothering you?" or "What's happening at school?" or other such general openers are most likely to elicit empty responses, as my friend realized. Not only are they too general, but they require a basis of confidence before answering fully. Such comes from long-term, daily contact. It comes from feeling comfortable in being with the parent. It comes from a solid history of a relationship where the child knows he will be well received.

That is to say, besides the time for talking, what helps most in having an open conversation with a child is trust. Can he trust his parent to receive his words without destroying him? Will the parent use the information to help him? Will the parent truly hear him and work in the child's best interest?

I mentioned earlier how my daughter's kindergarten teacher threw out a book Rikki had been making. When I picked her up from school, Rikki, with barely disguised tears, told me what had happened. She did not ask me to get the book. She did not ask me to talk to her teacher. She merely told me what had happened. She trusted me to do what was necessary. The emotions behind her words said it all. This was important to her. Something wrong had been done. It was now in my hands.

I immediately spoke to the teacher. With not a little indignation, I explained how the book was important to Rikki and throwing it out was not a very nice thing to do. We talked more, and eventually the teacher retrieved the book and gave a qualified apology to Rikki.

The damage had been done. The book was ruined. And the teacher had not completely embraced our stance. She did not see that all children's work is important to them; she only understood that this one piece mattered a lot to Rikki.

But Rikki had been given back some of her self-esteem. She had been listened to and understood, at least by her mother. The underlying message had been attended to. It was not just the book that mattered to her but also the manner in which she had been treated. Action had been taken. Her position had been supported. Rikki knew she was not alone; she had an ally.

As mentioned before, children, especially young ones, often do not know what is really bothering them. But conversation can give clues to what is contributing to the problem.

Hearing the underlying message is crucial. Realizing that there is more than just the spoken word requires knowing the child. We can know our child only by having spent time together. It is from having had experiences and discussions together that the parent learns when what is verbalized is the whole story. Another time, the words may mask what is really bothering the child. And then it will be up to the parent to know whether more will be forthcoming, whether the parent must draw it out, or whether the parent must decipher this puzzle on her own.

Popular in the media a few years ago was a study that claimed that what matters most in how children turn out is the peer group. Parents or other adults do not matter. It is, of course, not so simple.

Peers do exert an influence. In our culture where children are bunched into groups with others their own age – in school, in athletics, in extracurricular activities – peers will have an inappropriate influence. Children in such groups act like one another. The pressure to conform to the peer standard is great. This is true with any group. One heeds the dictates of the group because to belong is everything. It is identity; it is security. The alternative, going one's own way, is to risk nonacceptance and expulsion. Man is a social creature. Few are comfortable being on the outside, however much they are heeding their own call.

Not all children belong to such groups or to such groups exclusively. For instance, there are many schools that group children of a three-year age span into one class. Some educational systems have a greater span. Although I attended a regular elementary school, unlike most today, it had eight grades and was relatively small. These two factors mitigated the same-age peer influence. For instance, eighth graders both were looked up to and felt the responsibility of setting the standard for the younger children. And they were put in situations where they could fill such roles. Such is what happens when children are not limited to being with others only their own age. When with younger ones, they show the way. It is their chance to take the adult position of leader, to set a good example, and even to be a little boss.

Not every child rises to the occasion. There are those who seem to enjoy getting into trouble. Being with a younger child then gives them the opportunity to have a compatriot in mischief-making. Anyone with siblings has experienced an older one enjoying setting up a younger one to get into trouble. Despite such family experiences and despite adult fears, such set-ups outside the family are the exception rather than the rule. Too, such troublemakers are usually well known, and contact with them is minimized.

By and large, children enjoy being placed in an adult-like position and take seriously their role of guide to the littler ones.

In their turn, the younger children will heed the older ones. They want to be like them. They want to be accepted by them. They want to engage in activities with them. By participating with the older children, the younger ones feel older. Young children can be quite persistent in attaching themselves to older ones they admire. This is so despite what the older one thinks of the arrangement.

When young, I remember complaining to my mother about my sister, younger than I was by five years, who was constantly following me around and imitating me. I found it terribly annoying. My mother tried unsuccessfully to convince me to feel honored by the attention. Years later, I became my mother as my own daughter Rhiannon complained to me about her sister Rikki who always wanted to do what she was doing. Rather than complimented, she felt, as I had, annoyed.

Younger ones look to the older ones. And not all older ones are annoyed. It helps to get out of the more intimate sibling situation. Having a sibling who is always around can be tiring. Being able to choose the moments of when to be a guide to younger children is beneficial. The older one then has more control and is less likely to feel stifled. The older one can move in and out of such situations, deciding when, where, and how long to be teacher; when to switch to peers; or when to be taught, in turn, by an older one himself.

My family is fortunate to have in our neighborhood, children of various ages. Many of them easily move from one group to another, depending upon mood or availability. So Ty at 13 feels like one of the big guys when he spends time with 18-year-old neighbor boys. He will often also play with boys six or eight years old. Other times, he engages his peers. These interactions vary in type, too. Sometimes, it is physical activity – sports or outdoor games. Sometimes, it is quieter play – board games or Legos®. And some of the time it is just shooting the breeze. It is amazing how happy younger ones will be merely by being present around the older ones, just listening to them talk. They are learning, picking up cues, absorbing much of what transpires.

At a neighborhood party recently, all of the boys were gathered together. The youngest, a six-year-old, was in heaven. He was thrilled just to be part of the group. He said not a word but sat quietly, soaking it all in. So pleased was he to be with the older boys that he happily played their slave. Watching him only at the food table, one would have thought he had consumed a tremendous number of cookies. But, no, he was merely retrieving them for the older boys. (They did not terribly abuse his willingness; he did spend more time with them than with the cookie plate.)

Girls in the neighborhood also enjoyed such roles, younger ones seeking opportunities to be with older ones and older ones teaching the younger ones. Rikki, having been present during many of my art lessons for children, had learned not just how to draw but also how to teach others to do it. A favorite pupil was a neighbor girl more than a year her junior. All of us were pleased when, as a result of what she had learned from Rikki, the girl won an award for one of her artistic creations.

Children can learn from anyone. They seem to seek out especially those just older than they. Maybe it is because with a narrower age gap than between child and adult there is more rapport. Maybe it is greater understanding. The older one is not so far removed in time from where the younger one is. And his experiences are not so far distant. He can likely relate to what the younger one is going through, having done so recently himself. He can recall the frustrations or difficulties or feelings of incompetence.

I, too, could have taught Rikki's friend to draw. After all, I had taught many others. But I suspect it was a lot more fun for her to learn from Rikki. In between moments of instruction, they could talk as friends. There was already acceptance between them. There was already mutual trust and respect. It was a perfect environment in which to learn, to be able to make mistakes, to take risks.

It is a difference only of degree in such young child-older child relationships and a child-adult relationship where the two come together by mutual agreement. Children *do* look to adults for guidance. This is true for all ages. Contact with older children will inevitably demonstrate that even these respected older children look to adults for help in making their way to adulthood. Those adults may not always be parents, but teenagers *do* recognize that people who have already reached that point to which they themselves are heading can offer valuable assistance in their struggles to cope with growing up. Indeed, Francis Ianni, in his study of adolescents from various socioeconomic backgrounds, found this to be true. As noted in his *The Search for Structure: A Report on American Youth*, these youths sought out adults for information, support, and guidance. Another study mentioned by Kay Hymowitz in *Ready or Not: Why Treating Children as Small Adults Endangers their Future – and Ours* went further. It claimed that teenagers, like young children, need the support and security of their parents as they work on establishing their independence.

Of course, young children also are constantly working on becoming more independent. Yet they, far more than teenagers, hold their parents in an unfiltered, godlike image. They believe their parents can do anything and know everything. We bring trouble upon ourselves, however, when we try to maintain this position too long. There comes a time when children naturally discard their blind faith in their parents' complete competence.

Or at least, children try to see their parents in a more realistic light. They begin to realize our humanness, which includes faults, mistakes, and imperfections. But there are some parents who try to prolong their children's unrealistic perception of them as perfect. These parents claim they are always right – even when circumstances clearly show otherwise.

Our children frequently had contact with another family whose parents maintained this omniscient position. Several times they meted out punishments or restrictions based upon incomplete information. Even when provided with the whole story, which clearly showed the child had done no wrong, the punishment remained. To have removed the restriction would have been to admit that they, the all-knowing adults, had been wrong, had made a mistake, and were, indeed, fallible. Such could not be admitted. For if wrong in this case, doubt could be cast upon any decision made.

I am not sure for how long this family's children accepted their parents' always-right position. But I, too, was raised to believe my father was always right. I do not recall a single incident that revealed the absurdity of my father's position. But it did generate a reevaluation of everything he had said and done. Indeed, everything from him was then suspect. The pedestal he had created for himself was shattered.

Parents place themselves in such a position to be able to maintain control over their children. As discussed previously, such is not the only way. Having and giving respect works wonders.

So how do we parents handle this situation? How do we have the children obey, yet let them realize we are human with our many failings? How can we have them turn to us for advice and guidance when they know we make mistakes? Will children turn to adults who are not seen as perfect?

Well, of course! The danger is in wanting or expecting a child to seek out always and only the parent. For instance, my son currently enjoys playing tournaments with Star Wars™ cards. What I know about such games can fit on a pinhead. I would be a fool to pretend to be anything but an interested bystander. Those more knowledgeable on the subject are sought. In this case, it is an older person. When Ty was stuck working on a computer program, he sought a younger friend who he knew was familiar with that program. When daughter Rikki wanted to learn more about tracking animals, she found a group of people who are experts in the field.

No one person knows everything. Each one has an area or areas of expertise. They may be teachers who formally provide instruction. They may be neighbors or friends who willingly give their time to help another learn. They may even be youngsters who have explored certain topics in depth. To deny a child this rich array of knowledge is to limit the child.

And children know what they are looking for. They are not seeking infallibility. They do not need perfection in their parents or other adults. They are most accepting. The child sees the whole person with her many faults. The child focuses on only certain aspects of the adult. It is these valued characteristics that the child appreciates; these are what matter most. In *Talented Teenagers: The Roots of Success and Failure*, the authors describe how talented teenagers did not require "omnipotence or the possession of star quality" of their teachers in order to hold them in high esteem. What they did look for were indications that a teacher enjoyed her subject matter so much that not only was it an important ingredient in her life but it was also one she wished to share with others. This is shared passion. Have we been here before?

For most parents, this is not a problem. They readily help their child seek out such experts when the need or interest arises. What they most want to avoid, however, is their child turning to just anyone in matters of morals or beliefs or behavior. In these cases, it is not a matter of an absolute truth but rather a belief system. The parents have adopted or are part of a community that has certain accepted ways of behaving. Because these are not absolutes, differing beliefs can always be found that will challenge those of the family.

So how does the parent assure that she will be the one sought when the child questions those beliefs? Certainly, maintaining an omniscient role will be no guarantee as I learned from my own experience growing up.

But will appearing as one fallible also send the child to someone else who is seen as right? It depends.

It will depend to a great extent upon the atmosphere created at home. First, is the parent even around so that when questions or problems arise, she is available? Because teenagers are old enough to take care of themselves, this does not mean that there is no need for parents. There can be no interaction, no child seeking a parent, if the parent is not present. If the parent is home for only a few hours, there is no guarantee that the time of the child's need for advice or his readiness to talk will overlap with the parent's home-time. There is no substitute for being there.

This extends to other forms of communication. A cellular phone or e-mail can put a child in immediate contact with a parent. But it is nothing like being there. Given a choice between talking to a friend who is there or a parent on the phone, the more intimate interaction that is possible with the present friend will invariably win out.

Being present is not the only variable, but it is the basic one. Next is the atmosphere. How will the child's words be received? Peers are often sought because they are supportive. The child hears what he wants – that he is right, doing right, thinking right. Of course, this is not always so. It should be noted this is not limited to children.

Business executives, politicians, and people in authority surround themselves with "yes men." We all love to hear that we are right.

This point of being supportive of one's child comes through in Ellen Galinsky's *Ask the Children*. The author had assembled a panel of teenagers to answer questions from parents in a multinational company. What the parents most wanted to know was what caused certain teenagers to get into trouble. The teenagers replied that it was a lack of something — anything — to occupy a person. They basically told the parents to support their children in whatever interests they had. It did not matter what the interest was or whether the parents could relate to it. What mattered was that there was *something* to draw the child out of himself. In this light, support for the child then becomes support for the fact that he has outside interests. The focus is not on the specific interest, but on the child himself.

It is possible to be supportive without agreeing with the child. One needs to pay attention to what the child's needs in each case really are. What is he asking for? Is it for merely a listening ear and no comments? Is it for advice on how to act? Or is it for help and even forgiveness?

Many times an older child will want someone just to listen to him. In such situations, friends can easily substitute. But the parent still loses here even though no advice is desired. Missed is the opportunity for hearing what is going on in the child's life. It may be events that are disturbing; it may be forces that are affecting friends; it may be circumstances that will have an effect upon the child. Even though advice is not sought, what is talked about provides insight for further understanding one's child. If only listening is desired at this time, those other issues brought up can be held for another time.

Discussion is possible without attacking the child or his friends. This attacking is what the child most wishes to avoid. The idea of being viewed as wrong — regardless of the age of the child (or adult) — is what is difficult to face. It is even harder when others put the child in that position. Talking about concepts in general is more palatable than focusing solely on the child. The idea still comes across and in a way that is acceptable to the child.

Such rather impersonal discussions are more likely to occur when discussing what *others* have done. This is one way to convey a sense of right and wrong without bearing directly down on the child. Using such real life examples provides the means for establishing or fine-tuning the parents' code of acceptable behavior.

Such discussions were among the many methods our family used, for our children certainly tested the limits and, at times, went beyond. And we parents responded by letting them know that they had gone beyond. Consequences always followed. But it seemed that just as often what other children did served as the means for establishing proper behavior. Or sometimes, sadly, it was adult action that was the center of a lesson on what one should and should not do.

For example, certain adults were notorious for treating children as if they were of no consequence. The children were ignored by them or treated as if it were a tremendous burden even talking to them. Certainly, the children felt insulted by such treatment. But it was our family discussions that reinforced the idea that everyone, regardless of age or any other difference, should be treated with respect. It was made clear that, even though these were adults and they were behaving inappropriately, they still deserved our respect. Certainly, our estimation of them was lowered, but we, nevertheless, gave them respect even when they themselves did not give it. Such provided especially good opportunities for the children to practice respecting all people. It is easy to respect one who in turn respects us. But to give that respect to one who has only disdain for us is a far more difficult endeavor.

Living in a neighborhood of children and having contact with children in school situations also provided the basis for many discussions on proper behavior. Often the discussions involved why we thought the child did as he did. It was not so much to excuse the child as to understand that behavior does not happen in a vacuum. What one does is often in response to other events that we do not see, sometimes events seemingly unrelated.

There was a most unfortunate period when certain children Rikki spent time with became rather cliquish. It was a fluid relationship. Sometimes one child would be excluded, sometimes another. But always there was one who was in charge, one who decided who was in, one who had final say as to who was to be excluded.

It was my child who was often excluded. Another was also often in the same position. Not unexpectedly, when this other girl had the rare opportunity to treat others as she had been treated, she gave in: she excluded select individuals whenever possible. But I never allowed that from mine. Our family talked about this. We knew why, for instance, this other excluded one gave out what she received. But this understanding of her hurt did not mean we accepted it. It was still wrong.

We talked, too, about the one who was in charge of the group. Again, we did not excuse such behavior. It was wrong, mean, to exclude others in the neighborhood. It was even worse that adults, the child's parents, knowingly allowed it to carry on. Our stance was always one of inclusion. If playing with a friend, one was to welcome any others wanting to join in the fun. Our motto was "the more, the merrier."

What we did seek was understanding. Why did this one child act so mean to the others? Those who rule over such cliques are seeking power. They wish to exert control, which is denied them in other areas of their lives. So it was with this child. There was tremendous control over much of the child's time. It even extended to mealtimes. Everything placed on the plate had to be eaten, even junk food such as potato chips and even if the child was full. (It was no surprise mealtimes took so long for this child as he was forced to stuff himself.) It was no wonder the child was so desperate for control over some aspect of his life. Unfortunately, the part of his life he could control was not one that worked to my child's benefit.

My being around made a difference in several ways. The first was that I was aware of what was happening. Several of the other parents were not. Of course, those children who were the excluding ones had no incentive to apprise their parents of the situation. And most parents had no idea of the extent of the problem.

Second, I was available when my child was excluded. This had several results. I could talk to the other parents to get more cooperative play. But this was done only sometimes and, even then, only with one or two parents. Such appeals to the parents, I realized, were effective for, at most, only a day at a time. Too much interference on my part risked my becoming a nag and having a counterproductive result. More often, my presence meant that I was there to share my child's sorrow. We both realized anything I did was not going to change the situation in the long run. The clique leader would remain and would continue the exclusionary play. So I was there also to help my child face the reality. This was the way it was; I could not permanently change it, nor could my child.

Third, I was able to ensure that my child behaved properly. We could not control the other children, but we could ensure we acted toward others kindly and graciously. Their unkindness was no excuse for the same on our part.

Fourth, I was allowed to see how my child adapted. The sting from rejection was always there. Yet this adversity encouraged creativity in devising means for the others to want to join her. She came up with various games or long-lasting endeavors from which the clique leader could not keep the others away.

In this case, peers had a strong influence on each other. But the influence varied widely, based upon the parents' reactions. The second-in-command continued the exclusionary play as much as possible because the parent usually did not realize how often it was happening. While such cliquish behavior was not acceptable to the parent, she rarely took any action because she did not know how pervasive the practice was.

The clique leader continued in the mean-spirited, exclusionary play to a great extent because the parents allowed it. While the second-in-command's parents did not approve of such behavior, lack of awareness prevented appropriate action. Here, with the leader, the parents were aware but chose to do nothing to change the situation. They, at times, even condoned it by not permitting certain neighbor children in their house to play. By their example, they demonstrated that it was permissible to exclude some playmates but not others. Since power and control were denied their children in the rest of their lives, the children readily used this means as a way to exert some control, if not over themselves, then over others. One of the saddest results of this was that the child's younger sibling who had been most welcoming of other, especially older, neighbor children did a complete turnaround. Learning from the older sibling and taking cues from the parents, he soon, also, began keeping out some neighbors. A nasty "You can't play with us" became an automatic response before a question was even asked.

Peer influence is, after all, a handy excuse. If the child does not turn out as hoped, blame can be placed on others. What could the parents have done if peer pressure is so great? It is a fact, a given, that children will not listen to their parents and will, instead, turn to their peers. Or so some would have us believe.

The influence of parents is far greater than some will admit. It comes in many forms – by direct decree, by example, by silent approval, by ignorance. What parents do or do not do affects their child's behavior. It is certainly not the only factor involved, but its influence cannot be waved aside. And its influence lasts far longer than most realize.

One of my uncles, well into his seventies, still felt the influence of his long since deceased father. This uncle was making decisions based upon what he thought his father would have wanted him to do. Rather than having an internalized system of behavior, this man still looked to his father – or his memory of him – to determine what he should do.

In their desire for our support, children sometimes want only an open ear. Sometimes, they do seek advice. But other times, the support they desire is a much greater level of understanding. They know they have done wrong, and what they seek is forgiveness and help. It is as if they say "I am only human. I, too, make mistakes. Do not be too hard on me. Accept me and help me do better next time."

It is very difficult to admit one has made a mistake. First, there is the risk of appearing foolish, stupid, or bad because of this one act. Then, there is the risk of such evaluations being applied more broadly. So the child is not foolish just this one time but is always so. Instead of "What a stupid thing to do," it is "How stupid you always are." The one incident is then indicative of a general flaw in the child's character. Equally embarrassing is a further likely outcome: punishment. Embarrassment may not be an intended aspect of the punishment, but it can still be deeply felt. Ridicule hurts. Being held up as an example of how not to behave hurts. Knowing others are talking about one's mistake hurts. Outright punishment hurts as well.

This does not mean the child should be shielded from such outcomes. When one does wrong, one should admit it. And a natural result of making a mistake is that others will likely learn of it and may very well talk about it. If it is serious enough, the mistake, indeed, may lead others to make unfortunate conclusions about the child who made it. Such is a lesson of life. Our mistakes do have consequences. We can only hope our children will learn this from more minor incidents so that major ones never come into the picture.

What follows as a result of doing wrong may be difficult for the child to face. But that does not mean that those consequences should be eliminated. It does mean we should be understanding; we should be aware that it is difficult for a child to admit to mistakes. Turn this to oneself. Think how hard it is to openly admit to another or many others that one has erred. It is one thing to make a mistake, but to tell others of it is extremely embarrassing. It is bad enough to, say, make an arithmetic mistake, but to make an error in moral behavior is far worse. Who among us would not care that others talk about us because we failed to do right?

Think how much worse a child must feel. Remember, children are already well aware of how far from adulthood they are. They know they do not yet measure up. They know they are constantly making mistakes. They know they are still learning.

When young, each of my daughters had an incident of picking flowers from neighbors' yards. Each was old enough to know better. So each was made to apologize on her own to the appropriate neighbor. That was probably the worst punishment they could have received. Anticipation of what they thought would probably follow once they spoke to the neighbor was likely terrible and far out of proportion to what ensued. Certainly, the pretty flowers were not worth the embarrassment of admitting to another adult that they had done wrong. Yet there was extreme relief once forgiveness was granted by those same neighbors. The women knew well enough that the girls would never do anything like that again.

Admitting wrong, despite the humiliation, is a great cleansing act. Children want to be seen as good and right. When they are doing something they know is wrong, they are in a most uncomfortable situation: their wrong acts are in conflict with the image of themselves that they wish to project. To stop what they are doing is often not enough. They do need the forgiveness and understanding of the parent or other adult to allow that positive self-image once again to rest securely in place.

Many times, I have discovered that one of my children has done something wrong, only to be told by that child that there was more to it than I had thought. For instance, Ty was not allowed to play video games. This was so at home, at friends' houses, and anywhere else. Unfortunately, the temptation was too great. I discovered he had been playing them at a local store, which he visited for other reasons. I confronted him on his transgressions and explained that the store would henceforth be off limits. Despite the imposition of such restrictions, Ty proceeded to tell me more without any probing on my part. He confessed that he had also been playing at a friend's house. His friend's house was consequently also placed off limits for several weeks. Ty knew such would be the case, yet he still told all. He then had a clear slate. All was behind him. He could start over. And he had nothing to hide.

Playing video games is not inherently bad. It is not like hitting another child. But in our family, it was against the rules. Few other families we know had such rules. Opportunities for going against this rule were everywhere. Once broken, the rule was easier to continue to go against. How, then, to stop? Of course, it was in his power to stop, but he chose not to do so.

At the age of 12, Ty could not understand our reasoning for forbidding video games. It will be years before he has the wisdom and viewpoint of, say, his oldest sister. She had told us she was glad we had placed video games off limits. She had seen too many of her friends waste far too many hours (days, even) playing them in their addiction.

It is hard to obey rules with which one does not agree. That is not an excuse, for such rules are still to be obeyed. The child must trust that we, the ones imposing the rules, are wiser and do know what we are doing. On our part, it means we realize there may be more difficulty in the child complying with what he feels are onerous restrictions. It means that our help may be needed more here than with other "more reasonable" rules. It does not mean we go easy on the child as much as be more watchful and aware of how he is dealing with such rules. Consequences still follow, consistency is still maintained, and the rule still stands.

So with Ty, realizing that the rule was very difficult to follow when in certain environments, we placed those environments out of his reach. Being in the store was like being in a video arcade with a pocket full of coins. It was too difficult to resist the allure of the games. Once the friend's home was no longer off limits, he could visit with our trust that he would not again go against the rule. The friend knew about Ty's restriction, and, with many different options for play, he could readily engage in other, acceptable activities. And by being nearby and now more watchful, we could keep a closer eye on what Ty was doing.

One cannot discuss the idea of parents being present without directly addressing what has become the standard method of childcare in the United States. As more women have entered the workforce, fewer homes have even one parent home for the child. The one available to the child is now the daycare worker who, unlike a parent at home, has many more children under her care. Or, if the child is older and sometimes even if he is not, there is no one home for the child who watches the house alone.

Much of society aims to support this situation not because it is necessarily better for the children or society as a whole but because it serves self-interests. Politicians want the vote, so they cater to their (adult) constituents through legislation that supports parents working and their children remaining in daycare. The media want viewers and readers, so they present topics that show the benefits of children being cared for by non-family members. Institutions that care for children want to continue to operate, so they give credence to the appropriateness of daycare. And everyone, so it seems, has children in daycare, so the mere numbers support this lifestyle.

The practice of having others care for one's children has become part of a self-perpetuating support system, a glorified yes man. Parents want to hear that what they have chosen is good and right, so they gravitate to those institutions and people that support them. And that support is readily given because it ensures that those supporters will stay in business or in office. So on and on it goes, each supporting the other and neither side – parents and institutions – questioning whether what is being done serves best those whom everyone should care about most – the children.

There are, of course, studies that have examined the effects of daycare upon children. Unfortunately, the results have been all over the board – daycare has detrimental effects upon the child, daycare has no impact, and daycare actually benefits the child. Such divergent results only confuse the parent seeking helpful information.

But even if there were consistency in results, such studies could not help our children. They do not look at individual cases but at generalities. This does make a difference because each situation has elements that are so very different – the daycare workers, facilities, and rules; the child's home life; the time spent in daycare; the child's personality and maturity; and so on.

What we parents do need is much simpler. As has been said many times before, what we need is to understand our children. This we can do. We are, after all, the experts on our children. The solutions or answers lie within us and our children. A modicum of common sense helps, too. One does not need an extensive, expensive scientific study to reveal that a child will open up more readily if a parent is available for a greater, rather than lesser, part of the day. What a study may reveal is what my friend discovered – not so much *that* a child will talk if a parent is around, but the great *extent* to which conversation will occur.

To be these experts of our children requires awareness. And to be aware happens only if we are open to seeing, hearing, and understanding what is truly going on with our children. It means setting aside preconceived ideas about our own children. Believing "Here is my child who is wonderful and can do no wrong and can handle any situation with ease" will not help here. We cannot see faults or problems if we believe they cannot exist.

Nor can we see problems if we are not willing to do anything about it. Double-income parents must ask whether they are really willing to change their job situation. Two-income families are the norm these days. In order to maintain a certain standard of living, parents feel they must both work. But there *is* a choice here. No one is forcing both parents to work or to work the schedules that they do. They are choosing to do so. They are choosing to put a certain level of income as the priority in the family's life. So clothes, vacations, homes, entertainment, toys, etc., are placed ahead of a consideration that should matter more: time with those one loves.

For a parent to properly evaluate a child's situation means being totally open to looking at all that is in the child's life. This includes considering how the parents' jobs and schedules affect him. It means standing back and seeing the family members as an unbiased outsider might.

To look at the family and the children in that way would undoubtedly provide views from which many parents have closed themselves off. It is not even an outsider's viewpoint that is ignored; it is their own children's. In *Ask the Children*, author Ellen Galinsky spoke with many children about daycare. With parents not present, children would volunteer information to her that never fell on parents' ears. For instance, one ten-year-old boy related how his daycare provider would sometimes leave him in charge of the babies while she ran errands. He never told his parents because he believed it would only upset them. That is, I suspect, he felt they would prefer to remain in blissful ignorance about their supposed "good" daycare arrangement than to deal with making needed changes.

In Richard Louv's *Childhood's Future*, the author also heard from many children, while parents were not present, about the children's less-than-pleasant experiences in daycare. It was never the extreme abusive situations that the media have sensationalized. Instead, it was the little things that make for an overall unwanted situation. It was having friends constantly coming and going rather than staying for a long time as a neighborhood friend would be able to do at home. It was having toys someone else thought the children wanted rather than ones of their own choosing. It was sleeping on an uncomfortable cot rather than in one's own bed.

As the children got older and more distant from their daycare experiences, more stories leaked out. With such distance in time, the children even felt comfortable relating some stories to their parents. In one such discussion with Louv, a teenager described how awful he had found daycare.

> *I really hated it. The only time that I was really with my*
> *parents was like, at night for dinner during the week. On the*
> *weekends we were too busy. We had to do a lot of things*
> *around the house because we were never there during the week.*

There it is, that element of time that is surrendered in the pursuit of money.

But the boy went on and described some of the stupid things done at daycare. For instance, at naptime if the child was not sleeping, he was hit with a flyswatter. That was a new revelation for that teenager's parents. But as the mother relates, it is only now that her son is out of daycare that she and her husband are hearing these stories.

In my neighborhood, a former neighbor provided daycare for children in her home. I doubt any of her clients knew her two adolescent sons had burgled many of the homes on the block in order to support their drug habits. Nor did the children she cared for talk to their parents about conditions in the daycare. Instead, those cared for by her after school would just walk around outside as long as possible before finally entering the house.

Are these instances of blindness on the parents' part? Or is it just that they are not given sufficient information? It is really both, for the two are related. The parents do not get sufficient information because they do not allow it to come to them. The environment they create does not allow an open examination of the circumstances. As the ten-year-old boy told Galinsky, information about what is wrong or not liked about daycare arrangements would only upset the parents. He knew what many children in daycare know: daycare is a given. There is no point in complaining. The environment the parents have created is one that assumes all is well. Words to the contrary would make no difference. And should behavior by the child indicate that childcare is not in the child's best interest, that, too, would be ignored.

When children believe that childcare is a given – and, indeed, it is for most of them – they tend to hold back from their parents information that would otherwise cause their parents to question the daycare arrangements. The children believe no change will result. But they also fear that any changes that might come about would be worse. This Galinsky also discovered in talking with children about daycare. The children volunteered that it was better to stick with a known situation, even if they did not especially like it. Switching to another sitter might be a bigger problem. Why risk it?

Of course, for these children, the daycare was a given. It was not a choice between daycare and parental care. It was a choice among many daycares. If parents are firm in not changing their work situation, then there is no point in considering how it affects the child. No meaningful change can occur if the jobs are found to be a primary but untouchable factor. More likely, such would not even be seen as a force negatively affecting the child. For such families, the evaluation has been determined in advance; the job has no negative impact. This allows the status quo to be maintained.

This is not to say that parents should not work and should only be home for the children. It says, merely, that unless parents are willing to consider the possibility that their jobs affect their children in a harmful way, no true evaluation of how the child is doing can occur.

If the parents see that the jobs are having an adverse affect on the child, there are choices open to them. They can choose to do nothing. This says, essentially, that the income matters more than the child's well-being. Of course, in extreme cases, that income may be the main consideration for the child's well-being. That is, without that job, there would be no money for the basics of life – food, shelter, and clothing. But for most middle- and upper-class families, that is not the situation. There is, indeed, a choice, and to do nothing is to place the child's interests and needs behind the parents' wants.

Parents can also choose to do something. Jobs can be changed in a way to benefit the child. Some families juggle jobs so that at least one parent is always home for the children. Others have at least one parent working from home. Some parents work part-time to reduce the time children are in daycare.

After being a dual-income family for years, our family took the so-called traditional route: I, the mother, quit my full-time job to be home with the children. Yes, we made adjustments. There just is no way to cut a family's income in half without making significant changes. Vacations were not eliminated but took a different form. Rather than flying to our destinations, we drove. Rather than getting hotel accommodations, we had tents and sleeping bags. The number of meals eaten in restaurants became virtually nonexistent. Thrift stores became our haunts. All of these changes could be seen as sacrifices. Yet that depends. Camping was enjoyed by all. Certainly for the children, there was more to do in the woods, fields, and beaches than in any hotel room. Eliminating restaurant meals meant I had incentive to hone my cooking skills. Homemade, freshly baked breads became the standard at meals.

But those benefits of the change in my job situation were only icing on the cake. The primary one was the impact on the children. There was no longer the constant rush. "Hurry up" were no longer the main words spoken in the morning as the children were gathered for daycare or school. There was, finally, time.

There was time to plant gardens, walk to the library, make valentines for each friend and relative. There was time to watch ants for hours on end. There was time to sit and plan the next project. And, most important, there was time to discover one another.

This element of time cannot be overestimated. It not only gives the child the opportunity to do what he most needs to do – play without rushing or interrupting – but it also gives both the parent and child what is the most basic ingredient in a parent's relationship with her child. Without time, nothing can happen – no understanding can take place; no insights into the child's behavior can be learned; no discovery of what the child can or cannot do can be gleaned.

Now, there are those parents who will say, "Look at so-and-so's children. The parents both worked and their children turned out okay." But that is a narrow view of the situation. It merely looks at what is, rather than what could have been. More, it says turning out "okay" is sufficient. But, really, why should we be satisfied with mediocrity? That is all that "okay" is. It is nothing awful, but it is also nothing superior or outstanding.

Americans seem especially accepting of mediocrity in their children's performance. Studies comparing elementary school children in Japan, China, and the United States, as cited in *The Learning Gap: Why Our Schools Are Failing and What We Can Learn from Japanese and Chinese Education* by Harold Stevenson and James Stigler, found many myth-breaking differences. One standout difference that accounted for the poorer academic performance of children in the United States rested with the parents. American parents were found to be satisfied with lower standards of achievement in their children than were their counterparts in China and Japan.

Too many parents are satisfied with too little effort and too little achievement in their children. Going easy on them in this way is hardly respectful. It is hardly honoring the individuality of each child by letting him perform at a subpar level.

Whether it is academics or personality development, mediocrity is not a level on which we put our sights. Few parents, when talking of their children and the dreams they have for them, say that they hope only that they will turn out all right. Mediocrity is not what they hold as their highest hopes. Mediocrity is, instead, something to which they resign themselves later on.

But why? Why do the high hopes give way to lesser dreams? I suspect the reasons are many. For one, if the culture as a whole is satisfied with mediocre performance, there is tremendous support in keeping along those lines. And, unfortunately, such are the standards that are acceptable in our American culture. It is easy, possible, and acceptable just to get by. Minimal effort is enough. School standards say this. Parents say this. Children do it.

Also supporting such low standards is the effort required to go against it. It does take work. First, parents must investigate and learn what are low, average, and high levels of performance. It is not just academic standards where parents' expectations come into play. All aspects of a child's personality and development are considered. To hold high standards for academics and not care about how the child conducts himself otherwise is to do him injustice. Always, it is the best that we expect of him.

For instance, most people who talk on the phone will, when calling someone else, begin with "Is so-and-so there?" It takes awareness to notice the difference between that and "Hello, this is Jane Doe. Is Suzy Que there?" It means the difference between doing just okay – being able to talk on the phone – and doing well – being able to talk confidently and considerately. The former is minimal performance. The latter rises above that and recognizes that the person on the other end of the phone is wondering who is calling and not just who is wanted.

This example reflects a very minor aspect of life. Yet it is one of many little pieces that contribute to a child growing into an adult who either is just okay or stands above such a low standard. In truth, such little instances of social grace are very important. They are among the initial ones a stranger, whether a potential employer, future client, or a possible mother-in-law, uses to determine what kind of person the caller is. They give a quick snapshot view of whether the person is just another average Joe Schmoe or a standout person of quality.

Whether in academics, athletics, social interactions, or anything else the child takes on, effort is required to recognize what the standards are. Further effort is needed to enforce those standards. It is not enough merely to tell a child to do something; more must be done than that. The parent, first, must know what the child is capable of doing. It would appear from the Japan-China-United States comparative study of children that American parents think that their children are not capable of much. Or why hold them to such low standards? Are they possibly saying, instead, that their children can achieve more, but there is no need to do so?

To know what a child can do requires having spent time with that child. When significant hours of a child's life are spent away from his parents, those hours represent lost opportunities for the parents to know their child. It is by seeing what the child does in his play, in his conversation, in his mistakes that the parent comes to understand the child's capabilities, interests, and weaknesses. There is no adequate substitute for being there. Another adult may give a report, but many of the subtleties are lost. An adult watching over many children will not notice nearly as much as a parent watching over her precious little one.

To enforce higher standards means relying on what is constantly mentioned here: setting the example. There is just no avoiding this. "Do what I say, not what I do" will not cut it. If we, the parents, are satisfied with mediocre performance in ourselves, it will be an uphill battle to instill higher standards in our children. We must ask, do we demand as much from ourselves as we do from our children? Or, more likely, are we satisfied with just getting by? As always, our actions teach most effectively, whether those actions be ones we want imitated or avoided.

To rise above the mediocre, one must recognize the different levels of achievement. One must also know one's child and his capabilities. One must set a good example. And, finally, one must enforce the appropriate standard. This last step, seeing that the standards are adhered to, takes at least as much effort as setting the good example. It *is* effort.

It is not enough to rely upon others to do this. It is our responsibility. As the parents, we, before anyone else, must see that our children perform as expected.

Going back to the previously mentioned phone etiquette, I can count on one hand the number of children (and adults!) who identify themselves when they call us on the phone. It would have been all too easy to let my children behave in such a way. Instead, it took not only my own example in how to talk when calling others, but also my insistence on them identifying themselves. It meant, too, that I needed to be around when they made their calls. This did not mean intruding on their private lives. It was more just listening for their opening sentence before tuning out the rest of their conversation.

When Rikki was being excluded by her so-called friends, it would have been easy to have allowed her to do the same to them. Indeed, there were times when she would have liked to have kept playing with only the friend who was with her. When others, especially the clique leader, came over to play, the temptation was there to refuse his request to join Rikki and friend. But our standards were higher than that. We did not return meanness in kind. We did not exclude others. We did not give in.

When Ty was 11, we entered a Lego®-building contest. I say "we," but Ty did most of the work. His first effort was impressive. But only then did I read the fine print of the entry form and realize our mistake. Ty had used imitation Lego® pieces, and they were not allowed. The whole structure had to be dismantled. Understandably, Ty was not pleased. When that was done and the new one completed, Ty revealed that non-Lego® pieces still remained, hidden in the base of the set-up.

As the entry for the contest was merely a photograph and not the actual structure, those illegal pieces would never be seen. Yet I insisted on removing them. We could not claim to be abiding by the rules when we knew very well that we were not. Here, too, our standards were higher than such easily concealed dishonesty.

The final product, the third effort, was not only legal but impressive. Each reworking of the project had been an improvement over the previous one, and this third attempt was the best one yet. Others evidently thought so, too, for it won an award.

Putting in such effort and redoing a project to make it one's best is what we emphasize. On another occasion when Ty was just learning to print, he entered a science experiment contest. His first write-up took tremendously long to do even though it was only a page long. Even still, it did not look the best. So he rewrote it. The second time was not any easier or any faster. But it did look very neat. Ty was very proud of his work, especially after putting in so much effort. Here, too, his work was rewarded with not only pride in a job well done but also an award.

Of course, our efforts to do our best do not always result in prizes or awards. Nor are they the primary reason to put forth such effort. We do our best because our work reflects us; it is a comment on who we are and what we stand for. Certainly, my children's efforts have not always had the recognition that Ty's did in the above two examples. Sometimes, the work is not even for public display.

Some time after the infamous kindergarten-book incident, Rikki created another book. For this one, too, she devised the story, wrote it, and illustrated it. All was done by hand. I lost count of the number of times she rewrote the story. She certainly had a taste of what adult writers go through in taking an idea, developing it, and completing it in book form. This project that lasted many weeks for Rikki was comparable to one lasting for months for an adult author. In the end, she was most pleased with her book. It was not for any contest. It was just for her, and it was beautiful. Work can indeed be its own reward.

Other cultures readily embrace this idea. Stevenson and Stigler mention the classic Asian response to academic performance in their children: "Why did you not do better?" Even when the child achieves perfect marks and has done all he supposedly can do, so goes the joke, the parents continue with "But will you keep it up?" These are high standards. But they are not based upon the individual child. Instead they are general and based upon the best that can be done by anyone. If one takes the individual into account, the query becomes "Is this the best *you* can do? Is this reflective of the best that *you* are?"

Setting high standards is work for parent as well as child. But it is nowhere near impossible. One tries, examines one's performance, recognizes mistakes, figures out what to do differently next time, and then does again. This is effort, but it need not be unpleasant. Accomplishing is rewarding in itself. Doing better is even more rewarding. This is as true for the example-setting parent as it is for the child.

We parents set the good example not just in order to show the child how it is done. We do it, also, because we hold ourselves to high standards. The example we show our child is just the natural by-product of our efforts.

Some time ago when our favorite bakery started turning out burnt bread, I figured it was time for me to learn to bake bread. Certainly, I knew, I could do no worse than that bakery.

My first attempts were embarrassing. Loaves that should have been puffed up were rather flat. But at least they were not burnt. It took many attempts to get the chemistry right – the water in the mix needed to be a certain temperature, the air around the dough could not be too cool, and there needed to be a good balance between dry and wet ingredients. It was not enough merely to follow a recipe. One had to go by feel as basic ingredients vary in certain key properties. Not all "large" eggs are the same size. Flours are not all the same; some are drier or coarser or have higher protein content, all of which affect how they react to the other ingredients as well as to the rising process.

So the family suffered through my learning process. They saw that a failure or a less-than-satisfactory result did not end my bread baking. Instead, the mistakes spurred me on to master this skill.

In fact, this focuses on a major difference, according to Stevenson and Stigler, between how the Japanese and Chinese children view mistakes in school versus how their American counterparts do. For the Americans, mistakes and wrong answers are embarrassing. They feel they are indicators of their inadequacy or even their stupidity. They are to be avoided at all costs. But avoidance of mistakes does not necessarily cause the students to do better. Instead, the children learn not to give any answers for fear of being wrong. They attempt only what they are absolutely sure of. In contrast, the Japanese and Chinese students feel no shame in mistakes or in taking a long time to answer. All is seen as the learning process. Mistakes indicate where more needs to be learned or practiced or a different approach taken.

So it was with my bread baking. When the dough did not rise properly, I had to analyze many factors to determine what went wrong. Now several years later, a failure is rare. Almost forgotten are the many, many loaves that did not turn out.

My persistence was done not to show my children that one should strive to high standards. That lesson was merely a by-product. I kept at it because my standards are high. I want to do well because what I do reflects upon me.

Such actions are what speak loudly to the children. They are such an integral part of the parent's life that there is no need to draw attention to them. They pervade all that the parent does. Of course, such teaching by example works only as long as there is time for child and parent to be together. The child needs to see the whole process. It is not enough to see a perfectly baked loaf of bread. There is no connection between that end result and all that preceded it. It is not just the mixing and kneading and shaping of the loaf done a few hours earlier. It is the decision to take on something new, such as yeast-bread baking, and the many subsequent trials and errors, all of which happened days and months before.

The process is at least as important as the end product. Perfectly formed loaves of golden bread do not just magically appear. Neither do novels write themselves, nor do vaccines arise on their own. There is a tremendous amount of time and persistence involved. To emphasize the end result without also showing what preceded it is to do injustice to the process. It is an incomplete and misleading picture for the child. Effort, commitment, persistence are all involved. Such take time on our part. To give a true picture of this striving for high standards means showing it all, from conception to working on it with the inevitable mistakes to achieving the final result. Taking the time to do it cannot be avoided. A lecture to the child always to do one's best is a poor substitute. Doing is far more effective. And this doing does not happen in an evening. It is bits and pieces of moments over many, many days. Not every single relevant instance will necessarily be captured by the child. He will likely have more going on in his life than just watching his parents. But the more the parent is around, the more likely the child will see what the parent is doing. The connection will be made, and he will realize not only the importance of striving for one's best but also the effort involved.

My choice of pronouns may seem to imply that it is the mother who should be with the child. This is not necessarily so. Certainly, early in the child's life when nourishment comes directly from the mother, it is often easiest for that parent to care for the infant. But even here it need not be so. With breast pumps and commercial formulas, fathers can share in this role.

Regardless of the age of the child, he will want both parents to be there. Having substantial time with one parent does not then compensate for little or no time with the other. I previously mentioned how I became an at-home mother and had significantly more time for my son, Ty, when he was three years old. Yet he, then, had an even greater need for time with his father. Time with each parent was out of balance. He, at least, knew what was required. It just took his parents awhile to figure it out.

Another family's son, at an equally young age, felt more time was needed with his mother. Both parents worked. But the father, knowing how important it was for him to have time with the boy, spent much of his free evenings and weekends with his son. In contrast, mom-time suffered.

In another family, the sons actually said they wanted more time with their mother. This, too, was a dual-income couple. The boys were older than the boys mentioned above and, thus, more vocal and more conscious of their needs. But there is a difference here over many families in which both parents work and the children are under an outsider's care. This mother had not always worked and had not always worked full-time. She had spent the years when they were young at home caring for them. The boys knew this. They knew that their mother's work schedule was of her own choosing. She could work fewer or even no hours. The family income, of course, would have been lessened, but the family would have been able to handle it as it had before she had resumed work. She worked mainly because she enjoyed it. So, knowing their mother could also have chosen not to work, the boys vocally wished that were the case again.

Being in such a position, for any parent, is not easy. The choice is between giving the child what is wanted and often also needed versus giving the parent what is wanted and, likewise, also often needed. It is a win-lose situation. One party gets its needs satisfied; the other does not.

Until fairly recently, it has been rare for children to be in such a situation with their mothers. But as more families have both parents working, this has changed. It is not just that there is too little time with the father, as was the case with the "traditional" family of the 1950's. There is now, also, too little time with the mother. The time may be balanced – only a little with each – but the absolute amount is inadequate.

Such a dilemma may well be the reason so many parents are out of touch with their children's very real needs. If they remain unaware of the crux of the problem, that is, too little time with the parents, nothing will be done. They will not realize there is a problem; they will not look for the source of the problem; they will not try to solve it. All is well in their minds. Or rather, all is just as it is with millions of other equally unaware parents. The support for remaining clueless is there in sheer numbers. Everyone else is doing the same thing, so it must be right. Signs that all is not well are explained away by the media and applauded by the working parents. Children who cry when left at daycare are just going through normal separation anxiety. Boys who wet their beds at night are just going through a phase many boys suffer through. Teens who are adrift with no goals for life beyond today are just in a typical rebellious stage.

To look at their children and question what has only recently been accepted as normal is to leave open the possibility that all is not well. To be fully aware is, then, to see that it is not just society that is at fault. It is not just this huge, unmanageable and unwieldy entity that exerts total control over everyone's lives. It is, ultimately, each individual who makes society what it is. It is we, the parents, who make choices that directly affect our children. Good or bad, right or wrong, we make the decisions. When we choose our career or money or power and in so doing also choose to deny our children what they need, we cannot blame society for the results. As Walt Kelly's Pogo wisely put it, "We have met the enemy, and they is us."

Changes in society come about through individual effort. To wait for others who will first make the changes or will pave the way that the path may be easier for us is to risk taking too long and losing the opportunity to make a difference. Our children will be grown and on their own by the time changes will spread to those not in the forefront.

In essence, there is no good reason to wait for others to do the work for us. There is no good reason to accept conditions that are not working for our children. There is no good reason to put up with what is less than mediocre, with what is hurting us, our children, our society.

To say it does not matter because we (or others) went through similar circumstances yet turned out okay is to do injustice to the potential in each and every one of us. "Okay" is not enough. Unnecessary suffering is not tolerable. Disrespectful behavior toward anyone, child or adult, is inexcusable. Closing our eyes to what is before us serves no one.

We have choices. Options are always available to us if we will only leave ourselves open to see them. Our children depend upon us.

Chapter 13

Be Gentle

When the voices of children are heard on the green
And laughing is heard on the hill,
My heart is at rest within my breast
And everything else is still.

Feeling guilty about what we have done to our children is wasted energy. Guilt accomplishes nothing. If anything, it holds us back from taking meaningful action. In guilt, we wallow in the depths of self-pity. We feel awful for denying our children what they need. Oh, we are so terrible! How could we have done this?

We all make mistakes. I certainly have. That is why I especially like this quote from Fay Weldon:

> *The greatest advantage of not having children must be that you can go on believing that you are a nice person. Once you have children you realize how wars start.*

Oh, yes! With children we finally see ourselves as we really are. We think we are patient. Then we have a colicky baby that cries for hours on end despite our attempts to soothe and quiet it. It is then that we break down and know the limits of our patience. We think we are kind. Then we have a child who does one "bad" thing after another. After we swat him in anger, we wonder how kind we really are. We think we are giving. Then we come home exhausted from work to be greeted by our child who wants his share of our time. As we retreat to the solitude of our bedroom, we begin to realize that maybe we cannot give so very much after all.

Issues and feelings and beliefs we never realized we had rise to the surface. Totally unexpected and new experiences come our way. "Who are we?" we ask. "Is this how we really are? Is this how others have seen us all along?"

And what of our firmly held ideas that seem challenged at every turn? Suddenly, the way is not so clear. This raising of children is not so simple an endeavor. Certainty about what to do is gone. We are unsure and realize we can never know exactly what to do.

Add to the novelty and uncertainty the knowledge that what we do now to our children has repercussions years after, and we have a situation that can easily overwhelm a parent. How can we ever know if what we are doing is right? This is scary stuff. It is bad enough to see we have made mistakes with raising our children. But must we bear the burden, too, of having done irreparable harm to them? Oh, this guilt does not wash easily away.

When we are done wallowing, we allow ourselves some important insights.

One is that we are doing our best. And the more aware we become, the better we understand what "best" is for our child.

Two is that we work within certain restrictions. Some may be self-imposed – where we live, what job we hold, how our children are educated. Some may be a given – who our relatives are, what physical characteristics our bodies have, what natural disasters hit our homes. We may work to change those that are within our control. But there will still be times when conditions are not as we desire. It is within such parameters that we do our best. And the more we realize the impact these conditions have upon our child, the more we work to provide those conditions that are best for him.

Three is that we get another chance. And another. And another. One mistake does not end it all. Instead, each mistake is an opportunity to learn what we did wrong and how to do differently next time. Even should the unthinkable happen and our child die, opportunities remain. We can help others learn. Many a parent has used a child's death as the springboard for educating others that the same mistake is not repeated. The more chances we get, the greater is our opportunity to do what is best.

Four is that no child's behavior or character is set in stone. Our mistakes, our so-called best efforts, may do harm, but all is not lost. When we realize our error, we can correct it. Even if this realization comes so late that our child is now an adult, changes can be made. As an adult, he is now responsible for himself. If there is some aspect of his personality he does not like, he can change. Maybe we did make mistakes in raising our child. (Did I say maybe? Without a doubt, yes, we have all made mistakes.) But the impetus is now on him. Just as we grow and change and better ourselves, so, too, do our adult children.

We do not define ourselves or our children by past behavior. The moment is now. This is what matters – what we do today.

We are lucky. Our young children do not so easily give up on us. They give us chance after chance to learn from our mistakes. Opportunities abound.

What our children need from us is really so simple. They do not need video games or big screen televisions. They do not need expensive vacations in Hawaii. They do not need candy at every turn. What they need is simply love, respect, and understanding.

This much each of us can give.

Chapter 14

The Last Word

I hear America singing, the varied carols I hear,
Those of mechanics, each one singing his as it should be blithe and strong,
The carpenter singing his as he measures his plank or beam,
The mason singing his as he makes ready for work, or leave off work,
The boatman singing what belongs to him in his boat, the deckhand singing on the
*   steamboat deck,*
The shoemaker singing as he sits on his bench, the hatter singing as he stands,
The wood-cutter's song, the ploughboy's on his way in the morning, or at noon
*   intermission or at sundown,*
The delicious singing of the mother, or of the young wife at work, or of the girl sewing
*   or washing,*
Each singing what belongs to him or her and to none else,
The day that belongs to the day – at night the party of young fellows, robust, friendly,
Singing with open mouths their strong melodious songs.

- Walt Whitman

For as long as I can remember I have told my children that college is not a given. That is, they must have a good reason for going. Because they do not know what else to do or because all of their friends are going is not an appropriate reason. It is far too much time and money to waste without a purpose or goal in mind.

My husband does not agree with me. His stance is the more common one. That is, you should get a college degree. First, you never know when it will be needed, and, if you discover you do need one, you cannot just attain one on the spot. Second, most "good" jobs require one. Third and not so often voiced, people without degrees are not held in the same high esteem as are those with college degrees.

It was in light of such differing perspectives that the following conversation took place between Keith and my daughter Rikki, who was 12 at the time.

Keith: *"You should go to college."*
Rikki: *"But, Daddy, I don't want to go."*
Keith: *"Rikki, Rikki, Rikki! You can't get a job without a college degree."*
Rikki: *"Yes, you can. Look at Bill Gates*. He didn't get a college degree."*
Keith: *"Oh, Rikki! Bill Gates is one in a million."*
Rikki: *"But, Daddy, so am I. I'm one in a million, too."*

And so is each and every one of our children.

Whether our child goes to college or not is beside the point. What matters is whether we create the best environment to nurture that individuality. Each child has something precious to offer the world. Respect, honor, and love that child, and the best will come out. It takes effort, but, when the results are so wondrous, how can we call it work?

---

* Bill Gates dropped out of Harvard University, started Microsoft Corporation, and became the richest man in the world.

Bibliography

Star light, star bright,
First star I see tonight,
I wish I may, I wish I might,
Have the wish I wish tonight.

Anderson, Joan and Robin Wilkins
Getting Unplugged: Take Control of Your Family's Television, Video Game, and Computer Habits, New York, John Wiley & Sons, Inc., 1998.
This is a quickly read summary of what television does to the individual and family. It includes specific ideas on how to get the family out of the habit of watching and, instead, in the habit of living a fuller life. Real family experiences are given.

Bettelheim, Bruno
A Good Enough Parent: A Book on Child-Rearing, New York, Alfred A. Knopf, 1987.
Love Is Not Enough: The Treatment of Emotionally Disturbed Children, New York, The Free Press, 1967.
The Uses of Enchantment: The Meaning and Importance of Fairy Tales, New York, Alfred A. Knopf, 1976.
Despite the relatively new, public revelations about Bettelheim's character, his insight into the nature of children is still on target. Given that he was not the credentialed expert he made himself out to be, he may now be viewed as one of us – a layperson observing very closely what children do and why they do it.

Bills, Robert E.
Education for Intelligence, Washington, D. C., Acropolis Books, Ltd., 1982.

Blanton, Brad, Ph.D.
Practicing Radical Honesty: How to Complete the Past, Live in the Present, and Build a Future with a Little Help from Your Friends, Stanley, Virginia, Sparrowhawk Publishing, 2000.
    There is no mincing of words here. Blanton gets right to the point – be truthful always and everywhere and your relationships will be genuine. This is no less true for your children than for anyone else in your life.

Block, Dr. Mary Ann
No More Ritalin: Treating ADHD Without Drugs, New York, Kensington Publishing Co., 1996.
    Short and sweet, this book is full of reasons why diagnosing drugs for what some call ADHD is not only wrong but also does not work. Actual cases are presented showing how other causes are often at the root of what appear to be ADHD.

Brazelton, T. Berry, M. D.
To Listen to a Child: Understanding the Normal Problems of Growing Up, Reading, Massachusetts, Addison-Wesley Publishing Co., 1984.
    As the title indicates, Brazelton believes in listening to the child to discover what he is really saying. Unfortunately, what he calls normal is not necessarily natural. His premise is sound, but his interpretation of some children's behavior is not always so.

Breggin, Peter R., M.D.
Talking Back to Ritalin: What Doctors Aren't Telling You About Stimulants and ADHD, Cambridge, Massachusetts, Perseus Publications, 2001.
    If parents are questioning the ADHD diagnosis of their child or the prescription of Ritalin or similar drugs for their child, this

book has the information needed to sort fact from fiction. If the parents are not questioning such advice from the experts, they should – and after reading this book, they will. It is thorough, eye-opening, and well-documented.

Csikszentmihalyi, Mihaly
Flow: The Psychology of Optimal Experience, New York, Harper & Row, Publishers, 1990.
"Flow" is what happens when we are doing what we enjoy. Little children experience this all of the time – if adults do not get in their way.

Csikszentmihalyi, Mihaly, Kevin Rathunde, and Samuel Whalen
Talented Teenagers: The Roots of Success & Failure, New York, Cambridge University Press, 1993.
The authors looked at successful teenagers as defined by the adults in their lives and not necessarily by grades. The results are not especially surprising. But they are supportive of the importance of parents and other adults in helping teenagers make it through this difficult period.

Diller, Lawrence H.
Running on Ritalin: A Physician Reflects on Children, Society, and Performance in a Pill, New York, Bantam Books, 1998.

Frankl, Viktor E.
Man's Search for Meaning, New York, Simon & Schuster, 1984.
Written by a concentration camp survivor, this book is life-affirming and inspiring.

Galinsky, Ellen
Ask the Children: What America's Children Really Think About Working Parents, New York, William Morrow, 1999.
Sometimes children will open up to strangers more willingly than they will to their parents. Children know when someone

really wants to hear the truth. Galinsky is such a person; listen to what they tell her.

Gardner, Howard
Frames of Mind: The Theory of Multiple Intelligences, New York, Basic Books, 1983.
Intelligence Reframed, New York, Perseus Books Group, 1999.

Holt, John
How Children Fail, Reading, Massachusetts, Perseus Books, 1982.
How Children Learn, Reading, Massachusetts, Perseus Books, 1983.
Learning All the Time, Reading, Massachusetts, Addison-Wesley Publishing Company, Inc., 1989.
    Among his many books, these especially are full of stories of children just being children. His understanding of why they behave as they do and what they most need from us is beyond what most child development specialists ever see. Always, Holt was respectful of the child. Rather than seeing the child, as too many researchers do, as pieces to be examined and explained in isolation, Holt saw the whole child. His love, enthusiasm, and sensitivity toward children come through in all of his writings.

Hymowitz, Kay S.
Ready or Not: Why Treating Children as Small Adults Endangers Their Future – and Ours, New York, The Free Press, 1999.

Ianni, Francis
The Search for Structure: A Report on American Youth, New York, The Free Press, 1998.

Ingpen, Robert and Barbara Hayes
Folk Tales and Fables of Asia & Australia, New York, Chelsea House Publishers, 1994.

King-Smith, Dick

    Babe: The Gallant Pig, New York, Crown, 1985.

    This is an enjoyable little children's book, even better than the movie.

Kohn, Alfie

    What to Look for in a Classroom and Other Essays, San Francisco, Jossey-Bass Publishers, 1998.

Liedloff, Jean

    The Continuum Concept: Allowing Human Nature to Work Successfully, Reading, Massachusetts, Addison-Wesley Publishing Company, 1977.

    If I were to do it over again, this is *the* book I would use to guide me as a new parent. Liedloff shows how far we have deviated from providing our children with what they most need in life.

Louv, Richard

    Childhood's Future, New York, Doubleday (a division of Bantam Doubleday Dell Publishing Group, Inc.), 1990.

    The strength of this book lies in the author's ability to ask children the right questions and get revealing answers. Their responses show life from our children's perspective. Unfortunately, this life that we have created for them is not the wonderful one we think it is.

Mander, Jerry

    Four Arguments for the Elimination of Television, New York, William Morrow, 1978.

    This is a well-thought-out and thorough analysis of the negative aspects of television viewing.

Neill, A. S.

    The Dominie Books of A. S. Neill, New York, Hart Publishing Co., 1975.

    Neill is best known for the founding of Summerhill, a school in England which gives tremendous freedom to children. This trilogy (also published separately as *A Dominie's Log, A Dominie Dismissed,* and *A Dominie in Doubt*) was written before he founded that school and reveals the observations and experiences with children that resulted in the founding of such a radical school. Like John Holt, Neill is especially sensitive to children and understands well what they need. (A dominie is a teacher in Scotland.)

Pollak, Richard
  The Creation of Dr. B: A Biography of Bruno Bettelheim, New York, Simon & Schuster, 1997.
  This is the book that revealed how Bettelheim, one of the most highly regarded child psychologists of his day, had fooled everyone. His writings are still valid, but it is important to bear in mind that he was just like us – a layperson who came to understand children by observing them and interacting with them.

Roberts, Monty
  The Man Who Listens to Horses, New York, Random House, 1997.
  What Roberts did for horses, we need to do for children. We come to understand them by watching them. Once we understand them, we know how best to behave with them. Their cooperation, then, becomes a given.

Sacks, Peter
  Standardized Minds: The High Price of America's Testing Culture and What We Can Do to Change It, Cambridge, Massachusetts, Perseus Books, 1999.
  Testing and the results of tests lead to children being segmented and labeled, much to everyone's detriment. This book opens our eyes to the harm done in testing's name.

Schrag, Peter and Diane Divoky
The Myth of the Hyperactive Child & Other Means of Child Control,
New York, Random House, Inc., 1975.
The book may be more than 25 years old, but the attempts
to control children in harmful ways continue still.

Spock, Dr. Benjamin
Baby and Child Care, New York, Simon & Schuster, 1971.

Stallibrass, Alison
The Self-Respecting Child: Development Through Spontaneous Play,
Reading, Massachusetts, Addison-Wesley Publishing Company,
Inc., 1989.
Here is another layperson with insightful observations of
children drawn from her years of having a child's playgroup in her
home. She also brings in studies and commentary from well-known
child authorities, both scientists such as Jean Piaget and keen
observers such as Milicent Shinn (author of *Biography of a Baby*).

Stevenson, Harold W. and James W. Stigler
*The Learning Gap: Why Our Schools Are Failing and What We Can
Learn from Japanese and Chinese Education*, New York, Summit
Books, 1992.
This explodes many myths Americans hold about why foreign
educational systems are superior to ours. The solutions are not
what we have been led to believe.

Stoll, Clifford
Silicon Snake Oil: Second Thoughts on the Information Highway, New
York, Doubleday, 1995.

Time-Life Books Editors
*The Medical Advisor: The Complete Guide to Alternative and
Conventional Treatments*, Alexandria, Virginia, Time Life, Inc.,
2000.

Whiteley, Opal
> *The Singing Creek Where the Willows Grow: The Mystical Nature*
> *Diary of Opal Whiteley with a Biography and an Afterword by Benjamin*
> *Hoff,* New York, Penguin Books, 1994.

The diary is especially revealing in showing us a six-year-old child's perspective of our world. We can understand both how Opal's mother gets frustrated with her daughter's "mischief" and how Opal suffers, despite her good intentions, from never being listened to or understood by her mother.

Wickes, Frances G.
> *The Inner World of Childhood: A Study in Analytical Psychology,* New York, Appleton-Century, 1966.

This is yet another layperson who shows how children grow into healthy, happy, and well-functioning adults when we attend to their needs.

Winn, Marie
> *The Plug-In Drug,* New York, Viking, 1977.

Although scientific studies help back up her ideas, the bulk of this excellent book comes from observing and talking with children and adults about how television affects their lives.

Order Form

Qty.	Title	US Price	CN Price	Total
	One in a Million	$14.95	$19.95	
Shipping and handling Add $5.50 for orders under $20 Add $3.50 for each additional copy				
Sales tax (WA residents only, add 8.9%)				
Total enclosed				

Telephone orders:
Call 1-800-461-1931
have your Visa or
MasterCard ready.

Fax orders:
Fax completed
order form to
(425) 398-1380

Postal orders:
Send completed order
form to:
Hara Publishing
P.O. Box 19732
Seattle, WA 98109

E-mail orders:
E-mail your order request to
harapub@foxinternet.net

Payment: Please check one

☐Check   Name on Card:_____

☐Visa   Card #:_____

☐MasterCard   Expiration Date:_____

Name_____

Address_____

City_____

Daytime Phone_(_____)_____
Quantity discounts are available. Call (425) 398-2780 for more information.

Thank you for your order!

Order Form

Qty.	Title	US Price	CN Price	Total
	One in a Million	$14.95	$19.95	
Shipping and handling Add $5.50 for orders under $20 Add $3.50 for each additional copy				
Sales tax (WA residents only, add 8.9%)				
Total enclosed				

Telephone orders:
Call 1-800-461-1931
have your Visa or
MasterCard ready.

Fax orders:
Fax completed
order form to
(425) 398-1380

Postal orders:
Send completed order
form to:
Hara Publishing
P.O. Box 19732
Seattle, WA 98109

E-mail orders:
E-mail your order request to
harapub@foxinternet.net

Payment: Please check one

☐Check   Name on Card:_____

☐Visa   Card #:_____

☐MasterCard   Expiration Date:_____

Name_____

Address_____

City_____

Daytime Phone_(_____)_____
Quantity discounts are available. Call (425) 398-2780 for more information.

Thank you for your order!